THE COMPLETE GUIDE TO

Preserving Meat, Fish, and Game

Step-by-Step Instructions to Freezing, Canning, and Smoking

By Kenneth V. Oster

The Complete Guide to Preserving Meat, Fish, and Game:
Step-by-Step Instructions to Freezing, Canning, and Smoking

Copyright © 2011 by Atlantic Publishing Group, Inc.
1405 SW 6th Ave. • Ocala, Florida 34471 • 800-814-1132 • 352-622-1875–Fax
Web site: www.atlantic-pub.com • E-mail: sales@atlantic-pub.com
SAN Number: 268-1250

Oster, Kenneth V., 1952-
 The complete guide to preserving meat, fish, and game : step-by-step instructions to freezing, canning, curing, and smoking / by Kenneth V. Oster.
    p. cm.
Includes bibliographical references and index.
ISBN-13: 978-1-60138-343-3 (alk. paper)
ISBN-10: 1-60138-343-6 (alk. paper)
1. Canning and preserving. 2. Frozen foods. 3. Food--Preservation. I. Title.
TX601.O88 2010
641.4'2--dc22
                                2010050715

PROJECT MANAGER: Shannon McCarthy • EDITORAL INTERN/EDITOR: Sarah Ann Beckman
PROOFREADER: Hayley Love • hloveunlimited@gmail.com
BOOK PRODUCTION DESIGN: T.L. Price • design@tlpricefreelance.com
FRONT COVER DESIGN: Meg Buchner • megadesn@mchsi.com
BACK COVER DESIGN: Jackie Miller • millerjackiej@gmail.com

Printed on Recycled Paper

Printed in the United States

We recently lost our beloved pet "Bear," who was not only our best and dearest friend but also the "Vice President of Sunshine" here at Atlantic Publishing. He did not receive a salary but worked tirelessly 24 hours a day to please his parents.

Bear was a rescue dog that turned around and showered myself, my wife, Sherri, his grandparents Jean, Bob, and Nancy, and every person and animal he met (maybe not rabbits) with friendship and love. He made a lot of people smile every day.

We wanted you to know that a portion of the profits of this book will be donated to The Humane Society of the United States. — *Douglas & Sherri Brown*

The human-animal bond is as old as human history. We cherish our animal companions for their unconditional affection and acceptance. We feel a thrill when we glimpse wild creatures in their natural habitat or in our own backyard.

Unfortunately, the human-animal bond has at times been weakened. Humans have exploited some animal species to the point of extinction.

The Humane Society of the United States makes a difference in the lives of animals here at home and worldwide. The HSUS is dedicated to creating a world where our relationship with animals is guided by compassion. We seek a truly humane society in which animals are respected for their intrinsic value, and where the human-animal bond is strong.

Want to help animals? We have plenty of suggestions. Adopt a pet from a local shelter, join The Humane Society and be a part of our work to help companion animals and wildlife. You will be funding our educational, legislative, investigative, and outreach projects in the U.S. and across the globe.

Or perhaps you'd like to make a memorial donation in honor of a pet, friend, or relative? You can through our Kindred Spirits program. And if you'd like to contribute in a more structured way, our Planned Giving Office has suggestions about estate planning, annuities, and even gifts of stock that avoid capital gains taxes.

Maybe you have land that you would like to preserve as a lasting habitat for wildlife. Our Wildlife Land Trust can help you. Perhaps the land you want to share is a backyard— that's enough. Our Urban Wildlife Sanctuary Program will show you how to create a habitat for your wild neighbors.

So you see, it's easy to help animals. And The HSUS is here to help.

THE HUMANE SOCIETY
OF THE UNITED STATES.

2100 L Street NW • Washington, DC 20037 • 202-452-1100
www.humanesociety.org

Dedication

This book is dedicated to my wife, Joyce, who has faithfully stood with me through all of the challenges of life.

Table of Contents

Chapter 2: Equipment, Methods, and General Instructions **45**

Chapter 3: How about Beef for Dinner Tonight? 99

Chapter 4: Preserving Poultry for the Family 121

Chapter 5: Preserving the Pork   141

Chapter 6: Preserving Lamb and Mutton   163

Chapter 7: Have Some Goat for Supper   175

Chapter 8: Preserving Good, Lean Bison Meat   187

Chapter 9: Preserving Game Birds and Big Game Animals 197

Preface

The abundance of commercially processed food has left many people without a need for the art of home canning meats and vegetables. Home prepared and preserved foods were once essential in feeding families throughout the year. I have many fond memories of my family canning large quantities of fruits and vegetables that we enjoyed throughout the long winter months. A couple of those memories are still fresh in my mind, although they took place more than 20 years ago.

My wife's family still lives in South Central Nebraska producing corn, soybeans, and wheat. Each year, Uncle Neil plants several rows of sweet corn in a field near the house. Up to ten families would pick as much sweet corn as they can eat and preserve every year. One year, my wife, her mother, and our two daughters decided they were going to can as much corn as possible in a day or two. They canned more than 100 quarts of sweet corn fresh from the family farm that week. Besides the value of the fresh food that was preserved for months of enjoyment, they made a lifelong memory.

Several years ago, I was stationed at the former Wurtsmith Air Force Base in Michigan. One of the highlights each year was the annual salmon run up the Au Sable River, which flowed just a few miles from the base. One night my eldest son set out by himself on his bicycle to spend the night fishing.

He caught a 39-inch salmon. He must have been a real sight as he came through the main gate of the base, excited as he could be, riding his bicycle carrying his fishing gear and that big fish. He came into the house at about 2 a.m. and woke the whole family up. All seven of us stayed up and cleaned and canned that great fish in the early hours of the morning. That memory cannot be manufactured by the artificial technology of modern society.

When the opportunity was presented to me to work on this book, I realized that this was a chance to encourage families to spend time together and be involved in a valuable activity. Preserving meat at home not only provides your family with great food to enjoy, but it also brings your family back to standards that we are losing sight of in our fast-paced, modern world. I trust that this book will encourage you to get together with your family, dig out those old recipes your grandmother used, and make some memories preserving meat, fish, and wild game.

Introduction

Long before refrigeration became an important part of life, people had to find ways to preserve meat for survival. Most early hunter/gatherer societies were dependent on the availability of wild animals for food, clothing, and tools. As human beings developed the technology to increase efficiency in hunting and bringing down large animals, the knowledge and technology to safely preserve meat for long periods of time was also developed. Early attempts at civilization could not have been successful until improved efficiency in food production and preservation was developed.

Around 10,000 years ago, human beings in the region we now call the Middle East began learning how to domesticate wild animals and plant and harvest plants. The ability to develop control over food supplies is the foundation of being able to support cities and develop civilization. As the cultivation of crops became more successful, farmers were required to find efficient methods of crop storage that would extend the life of the harvested food.

In the early history of the human race, people learned how to preserve valuable food supplies to protect themselves against hunger and starvation. People learned how to dry fruits and vegetables by laying them out in the sun or on a hot stove. After the moisture in the food was removed, bacteria and other microorganisms could not grow. One of the keys to early food preservation techniques was the removal of water.

The discovery of using salt to preserve meats enabled mankind to go to sea and begin the age of exploration. Salt became such an important commodity that people were willing to fight for the possession of rich salt deposits.

Another important meat preservation process that early man discovered was the smoking and drying of fish. Communities that lived near the ocean, or near lakes and rivers, enjoyed a seemingly endless food supply that could be extended year-round with food preservation. There are 29 or more Pacific Northwest Native American tribes — such as the Cowlitz tribe or the Quinault tribe — that depended on smoked salmon for survival. Meriwether Lewis of the Lewis and Clark expedition recorded eating smoked salmon given to him by a member of the Shoshone tribe in 1805, far inland from the Pacific Ocean. Early techniques used to smoke fish were not meant to add flavor like today's processes. Smoking not only cooked the fish, but it also removed moisture and placed a chemical barrier on the fish against bacteria and microorganisms.

Ancient societies that learned how to preserve meat and other food items could develop and expand complex forms of civilization. The first well-known example of meat preservation was the use of salt pork and salt beef on ancient sailing vessels to extend the range ships could sail out to sea. Historically, salt pork was very important in the American Civil War, as it was the primary food of both the Union Army and the Confederate Army. (Salt beef was not as popular because of taste and because it did not remain in a fresh or edible condition as long.) There are many references to bacon from those days, but what they called bacon was just sliced salt pork.

Salt's value in history cannot be overstated. Our bodies need a certain amount of salt every day for us to survive. Salt can be found in nature; for example, salt can be obtained by simply heating and evaporating water in a pan. A company called Cargill harvests salt from the San Francisco Bay and other worldwide locations using sun and wind power. It produces about 650,000 tons annually, according to its Web site. Salt can even be evaporated out of fresh water from a lake because water flowing into the lake leaches salt from the surrounding land. Deposits of salt are also found in large underground mines or shallow, open strip mines. Some deposits are harvested by pumping water down a borehole and forcing the brine mixture to the surface where the salt is gathered after the water evaporates.

Long before the European entrance into the New World, American Indians were preserving meat in several different ways. The availability of game animals and fish in different parts of the continent dictated what these people were able to kill and preserve. Where fish were available, smoked fish became a staple. Large fish like salmon would be attached to pieces of wood and placed over a fire, absorbing the smoke into the meat. American Indians made jerky out of many different game animals and fish. The meat would be cut into strips, covered with salt, and set out to dry. The most interesting method for preserving meat was a food that was called pemmican, which is made by grinding dried meat, mixing it with ground berries, and adding rendered animal fat. This mixture may not sound too appetizing to us today, but it was a food with great value to early American people.

Early in the 19th century, the harvesting of ice from lakes and rivers became a major business enterprise. The ice was used by New England shippers to safely transport food products all the way to the tropics. When people began moving into the western areas of the continent in the mid-to-late 1800s, pioneers living in the northern areas of the continent continued this method of food preservation. During the cold winter months, they would go out to the nearest river, stream, or lake and cut large squares of ice and transport them to an icehouse. Straw would be packed around the ice to minimize melting as the weather turned warmer in the spring and summer. Ice packed this way could last through most of the summer. Each day families would go to the icehouse and get a piece of ice small enough to fit into the well-insulated icebox that was kept in the home. This is how food was preserved before the invention of electricity and refrigerators. Even today, people still refer to the refrigerator as an icebox.

The idyllic picture of an ice peddler with an old horse, pulling an ice wagon around town, putting ice in a box by the front door of people's homes, should impress upon your mind how important it was for people to learn how to make the available food last as long as possible. The preservation of food is the most important human survival skill that people can learn.

CONTINUING THE ART OF PRESERVING MEAT

Americans eat an indescribably large variety of commercially prepared meats every day. Grocery stores and convenience stores around the country sell huge quantities of commercially packaged beef jerky, pemmican, and smoked fish. The big difference between our modern, commercially preserved meats, and the preserved meats of the past, is the significant amount of additives and chemicals that are used to facilitate the preservation process. Five chemicals are commonly found in processed meats: sodium erythorbate, sodium nitrate, monosodium glutamate, maltodextrin, and alkaline phosphates. These chemicals keep meat from spoiling and turning to unpalatable colors, but are they good for our bodies?

Sodium erythorbate is a chemical compound used to help meat retain its red or pink coloring, and it is used to preserve freshness. Sodium nitrate retards bacteria that causes botulism and is essential to the meat curing processes. Monosodium glutamate (MSG) is commonly used to bring out flavor in preserved foods. Although widely used, some people experience short-term physical discomfort after consuming MSG. Maltodextrin is used as an artificial sweetener that is considered safe for most people but could be a problem for people with gluten intolerance if the maltodextrin was derived from wheat products. Alkaline phosphates are used to increase the pH factor in meat and to increase the amount of water meat products will hold. The level of consumption of this additive directly affects the balance of acids and alkaline in the human body. *A detailed discussion of chemicals and additives to commercially prepared meat products can be found in Chapter 1.*

With the advent of refrigeration, use of chemical additives, and mass transportation, Americans can enjoy fresh food year-round. Foods that are frozen or chemically preserved can be maintained at the same fresh taste they had at harvest because modern technology takes food directly from harvest and preparation and locks in the flavor before any spoilage occurs. The vast majority of people living today have no direct connection to the harvesting and packaging of the food they consume. The best reason for continuing the art of meat preservation is to have control over the chemicals that enter your body.

The average American will tell you food comes from the grocery store, but has no real concept of how it got there. Not too many years ago, most Americans knew how to milk a cow, feed the chickens, or slaughter a farm animal to provide meat for the family. Families would butcher animals raised on the land or game animals brought home from far afield. The meat would be prepared and preserved to provide food for many months.

These are family traditions that are worth all the hard work it would take to keep them going. Our technologically advanced world is in some way dehumanizing our way of life. Learning how to preserve meat would be a wonderful way to reintroduce your family to a rich heritage of closeness and maintain the rural tradition.

A major trend in the food industry over the last few years has been the natural food concept. Many food producers in cooperation with retailers are bringing to the marketplace products that are as free as possible from chemicals and artificial preservatives. These efforts do not come at a cheap price. Food producers and processors incur significant additional costs bringing food products to the marketplace without being able to use certain chemicals in the field and preservation process. The additional costs of production are usually passed on to the consumer. The best way to avoid paying higher prices for naturally prepared foods is to return the preservation process back to your home. You can really say you are eating naturally when you are involved in bringing food in from the harvest and preparing it for the dinner table in time-honored ways.

An experience comes to mind from several years ago when my family was raising chickens on a small farmstead in central North Dakota. Our children learned many hard lessons about life when the time came to slaughter and clean about ten chickens that were living in the barn. Many older Americans can picture chickens hopping around the yard after their heads were chopped off, and the chickens were dunked in the tub of scalding water to facilitate pulling out the feathers. Can you remember the smell of Mother holding the chickens over the gas kitchen stove to burn off the pinfeathers? All of the hard work that goes into feeding and caring for the growing chickens produces food in the freezer that is wholesome and well-earned. The goal of this book is to help people produce and consume preserved meat the healthy way.

Bill and Kay Tomaszewski and their children are very involved in hunting, fishing, and preserving the meat they harvest. They provided the following anecdote when they were interviewed for this book.

"We were called into a parent/teacher conference with one of our grade-school children. The counselor was seriously concerned. She explained to us the schoolteacher asked the child, 'What are the four seasons of the year?' He replied, 'Deer season, bird hunting season, turkey season, and fishing season.' The counselor did not appreciate our initial burst of laughter."

Farmers Bill and Kay Tomaszewski explain their response to these kind questions this way: "Our diet is healthier because our food is lean and free of contamination due to the fact it is produced here at our home. We are proud to be able to provide for ourselves. We make it a family event when it comes time to process, for instance, the summer sausage, the brats, etc. Everyone helps out, and we have a great time. It has been a healthy learning experience for the children, and we enjoy the hunting and fishing to supply the meat for preservation."

CHAPTER 1:
Basic Understanding of the Canning, Curing, and Smoking Process

This chapter is designed to help the beginner and challenge the experienced meat preserver to learn all the different ways that meat can be preserved. There is some interesting chemistry involved in the process of making meat safe to eat after a long period of storage. There are distinct advantages to each preservation method that will be discussed in the book. Hopefully, the material included in this chapter will be interesting enough to keep you reading and thinking all the way to the end of the book. Along with some basic instructions, general safety issues will be discussed, with more specific information to come later in the book. All temperatures in this book are in Fahrenheit, unless otherwise stated.

WHAT IS CANNING, AND HOW IS IT BENEFICIAL?

The process for preserving food in glass jars was invented by Nicolas Appert in 1809 in response to a challenge from Napoleon to find a way to feed his army. As the size and complexity of armies increased, it became more difficult to provide food when the army was on the move. The traditional method of an army scavenging and living off the land could not be sustained during long-term campaigns. When Appert first discovered the canning process, he did not have any knowledge of the science of bacteriology or food decay. Over a period of 14 years of experimentation using trial and error, he discovered that food heated to temperatures above 212 degrees and sealed in glass bottles could be preserved safe for human consumption for long periods of time.

Appert preferred using glass bottles for food preservation. Since the preservation process that was discovered was initially in response to a need to feed troops on long campaign, glass bottles presented a problem due to the risk of breakage during transport. By 1822, Appert had discovered how to store preserved food in tin-plated steel cans, solving the problem of food loss during long-distance transportation. Over time, the technology was developed to mass-produce preserved foods in metal cans. This is where the word "canning" came from. Today, only specialty food products are commercially packaged in glass jars.

To make it simple, canning is the process of sterilizing the container, preparing the food to be stored, and sealing the container so no contaminants can enter and spoil the food. Care in each of these three steps is essential. The jars used must be cleaned and sterilized to ensure that no bacteria can come in contact with the food that is being preserved. Different kinds of food require specific preparation methods depending on the chemical makeup of that particular commodity. The difference primarily revolves around the temperature the food must be prepared at. Modern canning jar manufacturers have provided the home canner with a special lid that makes it easy to seal canning jars. When the home canning jars have been filled with properly prepared food and the canning lids put in place, the prepared jars are set out to wait for the distinctive "pop" that indicates the jar is sealed and ready for storage. Canning jar lids also provide a means to indicate when a jar is unsealed and allowed air and moisture to enter the jar. Sealed lids are slightly concave, while an unsealed lid will no longer have a concave appearance but will be level or slightly bulged. Food jars that are found in an unsealed condition should be disposed of in a manner that will not contaminate other food being prepared in the kitchen. Spoiled food products should not be allowed to come in contact with any surface being used for food preparation. Dispose of spoiled food items in the garbage disposal, or dump the spoiled food into a trash bag and put in a dumpster outside.

Many can remember going to grandmother's cupboard or basement and seeing shelves stacked with jars full of all kinds of nutritious food, food that was prepared to feed the family through the long winter months. Preserved food stored in grandmother's basement or your own basement can provide you and your family with a significant measure of security and well-being. When the electricity goes out because of a big storm, food preserved in glass jars is not affected by the lack of electricity. It can be a valuable resource to get your family through difficult times. The safety of food stored for a long time can be easily inspected by making sure the lids remain sealed and by simply looking at the appearance of the food in the glass jars.

CASE STUDY: CANNING ON A 1930S FARM

Helen Ibsen Pyell
Westminster, Colorado
Member of Pioneer Family

A note from the author: As I was interviewing Helen Ibsen Pyell for a case study in Chapter 2, she revealed to me a wonderful account from her childhood of canning beef for the family's food needs. This account will be presented as closely to her words as possible. The hard work that went into providing food for a rural family on a homestead is very far removed from the life we live in America today.

Because there was no electricity or refrigeration in rural Nebraska in the early 1930s, the only way the Ibsen family could preserve the beef they butchered was to can it. The canned beef would keep the meat available for many months — even up to a year or more. The jars of meat were stored in the cellar under the cabin on shelves that had been built for that purpose. Other food items that had been canned could also be found on the shelves in the cellar. The cellar was cool even in the hottest months, helping to preserve the meat from spoilage.

The canning process began when the men pulled a steer out of the herd and butchered it. All of this work was done right there on the farm with the tools and equipment that were available in the 1930s. The beef was hung up and skinned out, and the butchering process started. The Ibsen family canned the entire animal, so they had to debone it and use every available cut of meat. The butchering was a long and laborious task.

The work in the kitchen had begun at the same time. They did not have propane or natural gas, but rather had a large wood-fire cook stove in the kitchen. Wood had to be cut, split, and carried into the cabin for this big day. The Ibsen family had a big oval tub to put the canning jars in to cook the meat and seal the jars. The big tub was placed on the wood stove and filled with water from the well. Each of the Ball® Mason canning jars were filled with beef as it was brought into the cabin from the butchering out in the yard. They did not have canning lids like the ones that are available today. Helen remembers one-piece zinc lids, which had a kind of a rubber-sealing surface. At that time, the canning jar lids did not make the distinctive "pop" sound we hear when modern lids seal on the jar.

As each jar was filled to capacity, the jar was set down into the hot water with a tool designed to lift and set the jars. Helen remembers quart jars, but there may have been larger one-gallon jars. The water in the steel tub was deep enough to completely cover each jar. The jars had to cook long enough for the meat to completely cook and long enough for the canning lids to completely seal. Because they were not using a pressure cooker canner, the temperature could not get above the boiling point, so the cooking process took a long time to ensure a safe food product. Beef-canning day was a long hot day in the kitchen with a level of work that most people today could not even imagine accomplishing. The jars full of good home-cooked beef were then taken out of the oval tub and carried down to the cellar for storage.

CURING AND SMOKING FISH AND MEAT

Curing and smoking meat represent a two-part process, so they are usually considered together. Curing meat in the home involves using salt and nitrates to preserve or save the meat for use in the future. The length of time that cured meat can be safely stored depends on the actual curing process, and the temperature the meat will be stored at. For example, chicken and turkey are usually exposed to a light cure so that the salt does not overwhelm the taste of the meat. A light cure does not use heavy salt concentrations, and the meat is not exposed to the cure for more than a few hours. Chickens and turkeys are usually smoked just enough to add flavor to the meat, and they are not smoked sufficiently enough to be stored without refrigeration. A chicken or a turkey that has been lightly cured and smoked will require refrigeration at or below 40 degrees Fahrenheit. The safe refrigeration time for poultry that has been smoked and cured in this manner is extended for up to three weeks, and it can be kept frozen for up to one year. Chicken and turkey cured and smoked sufficiently enough to store without refrigeration would be a very salty product that would not be acceptable taste-wise to most people.

Fish that has been lightly cured can be stored in the refrigerator for a period of ten to 14 days and may be kept frozen for two or three months. Since many smoking processes do not raise the temperature of meat high enough to cook it, the meat will need to be put through a curing process to preserve it from spoilage. Preparation of meat for smoking begins by curing the meat in either a brine solution that has been mixed according to a specific recipe determined by the type of meat, or dry cured with a salt mixture that is rubbed into the meat.

The availability of refrigeration will determine the level of curing that meat must be exposed to. If the meat will be used in areas where refrigeration is not readily available, it will be very important to follow through with the complete salting process. A point to remember is that not all curing and smoking processes cook meat. For example, cold smoking does not raise the temperature of meat to a high enough temperature to cook meat, so these products will need to be fully cooked before human consumption. A product such as salt pork may be fully preserved, but was not cooked prior to the salting process, and will still need to be cooked before it is consumed. It is essential to follow the cooking directions that are a part of the curing and smoking recipe being used

The benefits of curing and smoking meat

An important benefit to curing meat for use in the home is to maintain a readily available source of meat when the electricity goes out and there is no refrigeration. Home-cured meat might also be very important to your family in a natural disaster when normal sources of commercially available food supplies are not available. For some people, the greatest benefit might be to know that their family will not be exposed to some of the various chemicals that are found in commercially prepared meats. People who cure and smoke meat at home can effectively eliminate these chemicals from their family's diet. The following list describes many of the non-food additives that can be found in processed meats. Consumers should always read ingredient labels to understand exactly what they are consuming when they purchase processed meats. This list alone should be enough to convince people of the value of preserving good quality meat in the home.

Non-food chemical preservatives and additives in processed meats

1. Alkaline phosphates are chemicals that increase the pH factor in meat. The abbreviation pH stands for potential hydrogen. Alkaline phosphates are used to increase the amount of water processed meat has the capacity to hold. All meats except fresh sausage and ground beef contain this chemical. The level of alkaline phosphates consumed will affect the balance of acids and alkaline in the human body.

2. Sodium erythorbate is sodium salt of erythorbic acid. This chemical is added to meat to reduce nitric oxide in meat, which brings about a faster cure and helps meat to retain a pink color. It is produced from sugars derived from sugar beets, cane sugar, and corn. If consumed in excessive amounts, it may be considered a carcinogen.

3. Sodium nitrite is used in meat and fish to control changes in color and to control the bacterium that causes botulism. If consumed in high amounts, it can be toxic to humans and animals. Its concentration in

meat is regulated since it can form carcinogenic nitrosamines when exposed to excessive heat.

4. Monosodium glutamate, also known as MSG, is a sodium salt that is used as a flavor enhancer in processed meats. It is made through a fermentation process from sugars derived from such crops as sugar beet or sugar cane. Some people claim to have MSG intolerance, but scientists have yet to substantiate these claims.

5. Maltodextrin is derived from cornstarch in the United States, and it is derived from wheat in Europe and Asia. It is used to manage the amount of moisture in processed meats and can be used as an artificial sweetener. Wheat-based maltodextrin is a concern for people with intolerance for glutens. It is important to read the ingredients label of processed meats very carefully if you have celiac disease, as these people cannot digest gluten properly.

6. Antioxidants are used to slow the process of meat becoming rancid, which gives meat a longer shelf life. Proponents of the use of antioxidants claim significant health benefits from consuming these agents. There is significant on-going scientific research into the validity of these claims.

Additional non-food chemical preservatives and additives in processed foods

1. Aluminium silicate is a mineral salt that is used to keep dried milk in vending machines from caking. Although consumption of small amounts of this additive has not been found to present a serious health risk, reproductive and development problems have been found in experiments with animals exposed to aluminum compounds.

2. Amino acid compounds are used to fortify processed vegetables and are important to the human body in the correct combinations.

3. Ammonium carbonates are used in baked goods. These chemicals can affect the mucous membrane and can contribute to the loss of calcium and magnesium from the human body.

4. Antimicrobials are used to prevent the growth of molds and bacteria.

5. Antioxidants are used to keep foods from turning rancid and developing dark spots, as well as to aid in preventing the loss of important vitamins.

6. Butylated hydroxyanisole (BHA) and butylated hydroxytoluene (BHT) are used to inhibit fats and oils in foods from becoming rancid. They have been linked to several types of cancer.

7. Magnesium oxide is used as an anti-caking element in dairy products, canned vegetables, and can be used as a medicinal laxative.

8. Sorbitol is a sugar-alcohol based sweetener used in various food products. It has been linked to irritable bowel syndrome.

TIPS FOR SMOKING MEAT

After meat has been prepared in salt brine or packed in dry salt, the smoking process can begin. Smoking uses the heat of burning wood to cook the meat while adding flavor to the meat through the variety of wood being used. In America, the wood varieties that are used are hickory, mesquite, oak, pecan, alder, maple, apple, cherry, and plum.

Depending on how much heat the meat is exposed to during the smoking process, further cooking may be necessary before the meat is consumed. Meat exposed to temperatures of 165 to 185 degrees will fully cook. The best method to insure meat in the smoker is fully cooked is to use a meat thermometer and probe into the deepest part of the cut to insure the heat has reached all the way to the center. Hot-smoked meat can be considered fully cooked under these conditions. Although hot-smoked meat is fully cooked, most people will heat it thoroughly before serving it to their family and friends. Cold smoking does not expose meat to temperatures above 100 degrees, so cold-smoked meat must be cooked prior to consumption. Cold smoking is designed to give flavor to the meat, not cook it.

Cold-smoked meats that were only lightly cured must be refrigerated. The availability of refrigeration expands the range of curing and smoking options that are available in two ways. Meat that can be kept refrigerated does not need to be fully cured, but it can be cured to impart a desired taste. Meat that can be kept refrigerated does not need to be fully cooked in the smoking process, but it can be cold smoked to impart a desired taste also. Smoked meat being carried in a backpack for long hiking and camping trips without refrigeration should be fully cured and hot-smoked. If prepared and packaged properly, smoked meats will be a wonderful addition to your outdoor activity.

The primary benefit of smoking meat is the flavor that is imparted to the meat by the wood that was used in the smoking process. Each type of wood gives the meat a distinctive flavor. Flavor is a matter of opinion, so if you are just learning how to smoke meat, you may want to do some experimentation or find someone who is an experienced meat smoker and taste some samples of his or her work. The best type of wood to use is purely a matter of opinion and depends also on the size and capability of the smoker.

Woods such as hickory, mesquite, and oak give meats a stronger flavor than woods such as pecan and alder. Other woods such as maple, apple, cherry, and plum will give meat a sweet flavor. The decision as to which type of wood to use will probably be determined by what is available in your area for a reasonable cost. Purchasing wood at the lumberyard or a major home improvement store probably will be cost prohibitive. You will need to look for places that create scrap pieces, like carpenter shops or wood mills that may be in your area. The fun of exploration and discovery may even be an enjoyable activity for the whole family. The following chart will provide some guidance on which woods work best with different varieties of meat:

- Alder produces a slightly sweet flavoring that works well with fish, pork, and poultry.

- Apple produces a fruity, sweet flavoring that works well with pork and poultry.

- Cherry produces a sweet, fruity flavoring that works well with beef, pork, and poultry.

- Hickory produces a strong flavoring that works well with any meat that you want to impart a strong smoky flavor to.

- Maple produces a milder sweet flavoring that works well with pork and poultry.

- Mesquite produces a strong flavoring that works well with beef, fish, pork, and poultry.

- Oak produces a medium flavoring that should work well with any meat you choose to smoke.

- Pecan produces a nutty flavoring that will work well with poultry and ribs (beef or pork).

What is cold smoking?

Cold smoking is the process of using smoke to flavor meat without bringing the meat to a cooking heat. A good example of the value of cold smoking is the cold smoking of fish such as salmon. Salmon has been an important food resource for many cultures living near the sea for centuries. Ancient people had to fully cure salmon in a wet brine solution and hot smoke the fish to preserve it as a food source that would last several months. Since the modern world now has dependable refrigeration, cold smoking has become the preferred method to enjoy smoked salmon. Since cold smoking does not heat the meat to a cooking temperature, the result is a more delicate texture.

Commercial producers of cold-smoked salmon from locations around the world use a wide variety of wood types, imparting a unique flavor. People have come to prefer cold-smoked salmon from places like the Pacific Northwest or from Scotland. To protect the financial value of their product, nations such as the United States and the United Kingdom have enacted food labeling laws that require the label on cold-smoked salmon to indicate where it was smoked, where the fish was caught, and which smoking process was used. The exact flavor that is imparted to salmon, or any other fish or meat, by the cold smoking process is very important to people.

A good example of cold smoking today that people might recognize is cold-smoked ham. A quality, commercially cold-smoked ham may cost from $45 to more than $100, but it is a price that many people are willing to pay to get the flavor that the cold smoking has imparted to the meat. Curing and smoking are the reasons that pork products have the distinctive tastes that people enjoy so much. It is possible to find fresh pork that has not been cured or smoked, but most of the pork in the grocery store has been cured and smoked. Fresh pork that is slaughtered and sent straight to the cooking pot, and then to the table, would not have the wonderful taste that you have come to look forward to. This is why we have names like "cold-smoked ham," or "sugar-cured ham;" these are the processes that make the meat so good to eat.

The cold smoking process itself does not preserve meat. The initial preservation process in salt brine or a dry salt pack will still need to be accomplished before smoking the meat. The cold smoking process can take several days or even weeks, depending on how deeply you desire the smoke to penetrate the meat. The ideal temperature for cold smoking meat or fish is 80 degrees or lower, and certainly never above 100 degrees. There is a dangerous temperature zone you must be aware of when cold smoking. In the temperature range between 100 and 140 degrees, dangerous bacteria such as salmonella can grow and multiply. These bacteria are not killed until cooking temperatures rise above 140 degrees. Cold smokers are not designed to heat meat to temperatures that high. *A chart that provides a list of safe cooking temperatures for different kinds of meat is included in the middle of Chapter 2.* The important thing to remember is that fish and meat that are cold smoked will need to be cooked to the proper safe temperature when the time comes for consumption.

THINK ABOUT FOOD SAFETY AS A FAMILY SAFETY ISSUE

Foodborne illnesses are serious issues to consider when preserving meat and fish at home. *A chart of the most common foodborne illnesses has been included at the end of this chapter.* Since the bacterium that cause foodborne disease and illness are commonly found in the animals that enter the slaughterhouse, commercially prepared foods must meet strict safety regulations that have been established by the Food and Drug Administration (FDA). People who hunt and fish, or people who raise animals on their own property for slaughter, need to follow the same safety standards that have been established for commercial food producers.

Fish and meat that reach our dinner table have been monitored for safety from the farm or hatchery, through the slaughterhouse, through the packing facility, and all the way through the retail distribution system. Even after all of the inspections, tainted food still makes it through the system occasionally and onto our dinner tables. This is why it is so vitally important for the person preserving food for consumption in the home to know exactly what the safety rules are. The first place to begin is to look at the chemistry that goes on behind the scenes.

Common foodborne diseases

1. Campylobacter is found in the intestines of healthy birds. This bacterial pathogen is almost always found in uncooked poultry of any variety. The symptoms of the illness it causes will include fever, diarrhea, and abdominal cramps. Humans contract this disease by eating raw or undercooked chicken and other poultry. Additionally, other foods are infected when they come in contact with juices dripping from affected uncooked chicken and poultry. When handling raw poultry, it is essential to contain drippings from the bird and sanitize any kitchen surfaces uncooked poultry juices have dripped on.

2. Salmonella is a bacteria found in the intestines of birds, reptiles, and mammals. Symptoms of this disease may include fever, diarrhea, and abdominal cramps. People with weakened immune systems are particularly susceptible to this disease invading their bloodstream and causing life-threatening infections.

3.   E. coli O157:H7 is the most common type of the E. coli bacteria. It is a bacterial pathogen present in cattle and other animals. Humans are infected when food or water has come in contact with very small amounts of feces. This disease may cause bloody diarrhea and painful abdominal cramps with very little fever. In rare cases, it can cause a related complication called hemolytic uremic syndrome (HUS), which will not appear until several weeks after the initial symptoms caused by E. coli. The most serious problem HUS can cause is kidney failure. Again, the best precaution is proper food handling procedures and keeping slaughtered meat away from animal waste products.

4.   Calicivirus or Norwalk-like viruses cause a very common form of foodborne illness called gastroenteritis. This disease is rarely diagnosed because most labs do not have the necessary tests available. This disease causes acute gastrointestinal illness with vomiting and diarrhea. The disease is usually over in two days for most people. This disease is passed from person to person through kitchen workers handling food products with unwashed hands.

The chemistry behind meat preservation

Many interesting and curious chemical interactions take place when the meat preservation process starts. Conversely, if meat and fish are not preserved, chemical processes quickly lead to spoilage and disintegration of the product. This may not be a very pleasant process to consider, but it is important to understand so that you can keep your family safe when consuming the foods that are preserved in your home. Bacteria are very small organisms that you must use a microscope to see. Bacterium begins working on meat and fish just as soon as the animal dies of natural causes or is slaughtered. Since many destructive bacteria are found on the skin or in the intestines, incomplete or sloppy slaughtering and cleaning procedures can accelerate the spoilage of the meat or fish. The following chart provides some ideas and precautions to observe when slaughtering and butchering animals for human consumption.

Slaughtering and butchering meat safety precautions

1. Never harvest an animal for human consumption that is obviously sick.

2. When cleaning or field dressing an animal, never allow the contents of the intestines or bladder to come in contact with the meat.

3. Deer harvested in states where chronic wasting disease (CWD) is known to exist must be tested before the meat is butchered for human consumption. CWD is a neurological condition that affects deer and elk and causes a deterioration of body condition with behavioral problems and leads to death. Although there is no evidence that the disease has been transmitted to humans, the possibility does exist. When butchering in areas like Colorado, Utah, Wyoming, and other Midwestern states, do not allow any spinal fluid or brain tissue to come in contact with the meat until after the animal has been tested and declared free of CWD. The brochure published by the state game and fish department that lists hunting regulations will inform hunters if CWD infected animals are present in the state. The game and fish department also has information on laboratories that can test for the presence of this disease.

4. When butchering an animal, always be on the lookout for any sign that the animal is sick and the meat may not be safe for human consumption. Sick animals will act strangely, look weak, and have

deteriorated body mass. Normally healthy animals will run from contact with people, but sick animals may be overly aggressive or seem to be seeking assistance with their abnormality.

5.   Do not hang the carcass up for aging for long periods of time when temperatures are above 50 degrees Fahrenheit. In any case, it is not recommended to hang the carcass for more than a few days. While the carcass is hanging, keep dirt, dust, and rodents away from the meat.

6.   During slaughtering and butchering, it is recommended that anyone handling the meat use protective gloves as a preventative measure against spreading disease.

7.   When cleaning fish, do not return the internal organs to the water the fish came from.

8.   If fish or birds are cleaned in the kitchen, ensure that all waste materials are properly disposed of and counters and sinks are sanitized to prevent the spread of disease. To dispose of unwanted animal parts, place the unwanted items in a plastic trash bag and tie the bag closed securely. Take the bag outside and place in a trash container or dumpster. If you run unwanted parts down the disposal, you will need to ensure that all parts are flushed clear, and you should sanitize the disposal with a chlorine bleach solution.

Enzymes are important elements in the biological processes that make life on earth possible. Enzymes are proteins that facilitate chemical and biological processes in the body. They can be described as the workmen in cells that break down nutrients providing the energy needed to fuel life. After an animal dies, the enzymes in the body continue to work, reducing biological components down to smaller elements. The actions of the bacteria and enzymes will bring about a change of color in the meat and the smell of spoilage.

A third chemical process in the decaying of meat and fish is the oxidation of fat as it comes into contact with the air. Oxidation is easily defined as a process of reduction, or the transfer of electrons from one element to another. During oxidation, electrons from the fatty material in meat transfer to the oxygen the meat is exposed to. When fatty pieces of meat are left in contact with oxygen over a long period of time, the meat will develop a very bad smell. This smell signifies that the meat is turning rancid. Because of this chemical process, meat that is used for drying should always be of a leaner cut.

Meat and fish preservation techniques are designed to inhibit the decaying process for as long a period of time as possible. Some preservation techniques even enhance fresh taste and appearance. To the extent of the material covered by this book, techniques that inhibit decay in meat and fish are heat, drying and curing, refrigeration and freezing, the use of sugars, salts, and nitrates. Commercial meat-processing companies use several other chemical preservatives that were discussed earlier. Commercially applied food preservation chemicals are not readily available to the general public and are not necessary in home food preservation projects, since these products are not being mass-produced for sale to the consumer.

Heating food prior to consumption destroys the biological and chemical processes that lead to spoilage. Heating food to the proper temperature kills dangerous bacteria that lead to food poisoning. Of all the preservation methods available, heating food to preserve it for later use is the easiest and most cost-effective way to prepare meat and fish. Try to imagine what life would be like without the aid of fire in your everyday life.

Drying and curing meat and fish removes moisture that microorganisms need to live and develop. Dried and cured meat can be kept safely in a refrigerator for up to three weeks. Refrigerating below 40 degrees and bringing meat down to freezing temperatures stops bacteria from growing. The sugar-curing process increases the temperature of the food to temperatures higher than microbiological organisms, such as the ones described earlier in this chapter, can survive. Sugar curing has the benefit of adding wonderful flavor to meat such as pork. The other side of curing is the use of salt and nitrates. Bacteria cannot live in meats that have been soaked in salt brine or dry packed in salt in a curing box. In high concentrations, salt is toxic to bacteria.

General understanding of sanitation rules

The elimination of pathogens that cause foodborne illnesses is the reason for adhering to strict sanitation rules when preserving meat and fish. It takes very little contamination to cause spoilage of the meat you have worked so hard to put up for your family's enjoyment and nutrition. Sanitation begins with the meat product itself. If you have gone into the field and harvested an animal or went fishing and caught a great fish, field dressing and cleaning should be done with great care and clean water. Most states no longer allow fish to be cleaned in the body of water they were caught in because people in the past have left a dirty mess that someone else had to be paid to clean up.

Tables and counters used as working surfaces should be sanitized with cleaners that have been certified safe around food preparation processes. The most effective sanitizing agent is still a chlorine bleach solution. Bacterial organisms, such as E. coli and salmonella from the intestinal tract, can contaminate meat and fish if proper handling procedures were not followed when the animal was slaughtered and cleaned. These disease-causing organisms can be transferred to non-contaminated products if working surfaces are not properly cleaned between pieces of meat. If you process your wild game in the garage or out on the porch, you will still need to ensure that all surfaces that come in contact with the meat have been sanitized.

The following chart by All QA Products provides excellent information on sanitation procedures to keep a work area sanitary and safe from contaminants that could harm your family.

How to mix and use bleach solutions

Chart courtesy of All QA Products

Normally, 1 tablespoon of concentrated bleach per gallon of water at room temperature is considered to be the equivalent of 200 parts per million (PPM). This is the standard for cleaning food preparation surfaces.

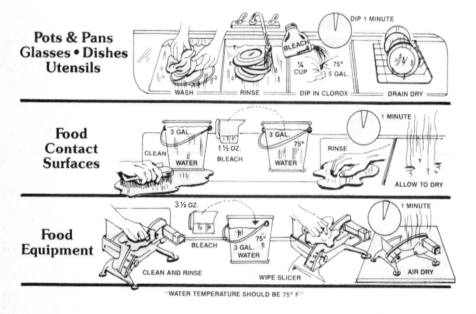

As you can see in these simplified instructions, there are some constant procedures.

- First, the temperature has to be right (hotter temperatures decrease the effectiveness of bleach solutions).

- Second, the time of exposure has to be at least one minute for a bacterial kill.

- Third, and perhaps most important, the concentration of chlorine must be adequate.

Here is a guideline for mixing bleach solutions:

Sanitizing activity	Ratio
Pots, pans, dishes, and utensils	2 oz. / 5 gal (about 0.3%)
Food contact surfaces	1.5 oz. / 3 gal. (About 0.4%)
Food processing equipment	3.5 oz. / 3 gal. (About 10%)

Sanitation concerns also apply to all the utensils being used to prepare your meat or fish. Cross contamination of meat products from unsanitary use of food processing equipment is a valid concern. All of this discussion of sanitation and cleaning may seem extreme, but the next time you hear a report on the news about someone getting sick from the food they have eaten, remember what you have read in this book.

The final part of this discussion on sanitation is canning jars and lids. Please do not assume that those new canning jars and lids you just purchased are clean and ready for use right out of the box. Those jars may still contain some residue from the manufacturing process and any contaminants that were picked up in shipping. Just think how terrible it would be if all of your hard work canning healthy food was spoiled and ruined for use because you sealed jars that were not properly cleaned.

Please follow all the cleaning instructions that came with that box of new jars you purchased at the hardware store. If you are using used jars and do not have cleaning instructions, just remember that the jars, lids, and metal band should be thoroughly cleaned with hot water and soap. If you have a dishwasher, that would be the best place to clean your canning equipment. Canning jars being used for meat do not need to be sterilized separately because they will be sterilized along with the meat in the canning process. Canning jars that are used for other foods such as jams, jellies, and pickled products that are processed for less than ten minutes and are not prepared in a pressure cooker canner do need to be sterilized separately.

CHAPTER 2:
Equipment, Methods, and General Instructions

This chapter is not designed to provide an exhaustive description and list of every imaginable brand and type of equipment used in the preservation of different kinds of meat and fish. There should be sufficient information presented on different kinds of equipment that you will be able to understand what equipment you need to preserve the specific type of meat or fish you are interested in. As different recipes are presented throughout the book, you will need to refer back to this chapter occasionally, so try to remember what you are reading and how to find the information you need.

FREEZING APPLIANCES, EQUIPMENT, AND SUPPLIES

Because most people have access to a refrigerator, kitchen stove, and a freezer, the simplest method for preserving meat and fish is to cook it and put it in the freezer. Simple freezing projects, like bringing a package of meat home from the grocery store and dividing it up into portions that the family can use at a single meal, do not require a long list of complicated instructions or equipment. All that is needed is a clean place to cut the meat, a sharp knife, and some freezer bags or plastic containers to put the meat in. This size of a project is just about right for those of us who like to enjoy good food with minimum work.

There is some controversy about the ability to preserve or enhance the freshness of meat or fish products by "fast freezing" them. Fast freezing food means to bring the food down to extremely cold temperatures immediately after it is cooked and packaged. Fifty percent or more of the seafood that is caught is fast frozen in freezing equipment that uses liquid nitrogen at about -320 degrees. Immediately fast freezing fresh food products in this manner not only stops bacterial growth, but it also preserves the food in its fresh condition for a longer period of time than conventional freezing methods. Other commercial processes exist that accomplish the same ends, but these results are obviously not possible with the freezer in your home since most in-home freezers only bring food down to about -18° F. Additionally, home freezers take a little time to get the food down to the lowest temperature they possibly can. The only way for the home preserver to accomplish anything close to this process would be to make arrangements with a local locker plant.

Many people who read this book may not be familiar with what a meat locker plant is. With the diminishing number of people raising animals at home to supply meat for their family, locker plants are slowly disappearing. The locker plant is the place people bring the steer they have been raising for slaughter or the game they have harvested for butchering and processing. Some may call this a butcher shop; however, a locker plant not only butchers animal carcasses, but it also provides storage lockers for people who have large quantities of meat that needs to be kept frozen. The freezers at a locker plant are much more efficient than those found in the average home, so the closest the home preserver can get to fast freezing is to bring their meat products to a locker plant.

The quick freezing and fast freezing processes that commercial meat processing companies are able to use are not realistic options for home meat preservers. You can use a freezer thermometer to determine just exactly how cold of a temperature your freezer will reach. If you are going to purchase a new freezer, pay close attention to the specifications provided by the manufacturer. If the freezer specifications show the freezer is only going to reach -8 degrees, for example, this would not be the best freezer for long-term storage of meat products. Remember that fast freezing to very cold temperatures freezes food without creating large ice crystals. Most people have probably tasted ice cream that had not been frozen properly, and the milk has turned to crystals, ruining the texture and taste of the product. People who want to preserve meat in a freezer for six months or more need to use a freezer that is capable of holding the product consistently at the lowest possible temperature. Meat stored in freezers that do not keep the product at a constant temperature should not be stored for more than six months. Remember that even if your freezer reaches -18 degrees, every time you open the door, the temperature in the storage compartment rises and must be brought back down to the lowest temperature again over a period of time. For the person who is going to store large quantities of meat for over six months, using the cold storage facilities at a locker plant may be the best option.

A reality check would be good at this point. Commercial food processors are preparing their product to be shipped all across the country and cannot absolutely control all of the conditions the product may encounter, so the product must be frozen to standards that exceed home freezing expectations. Commercial meat handling standards begin at the processing plant. Meat processing facilities are rigorously inspected for safe and sanitary handling of animal carcasses and finished meat products. Meat-handling standards also are concerned with any substance that is artificially added to the product and ensuring meat product labels accurately reflect the contents of the finished product. Meat-handling regulations also specify that fresh and frozen products should be maintained at the proper temperature throughout storage, transportation, and presentation in the retail outlet. Although food frozen for commercial sale is packaged with expiration dates, manufacturers cannot be sure the food will be consumed by the expected expiration date. Consumers have the responsibility to protect themselves by not using meat products that have been in storage beyond the date that is printed on the package. Commercial packaging, freezing, and distribution standards must meet the highest possible food safety expectations.

Your home freezer will do just fine as long as it is in good working order and as long as you have prepared your meat and fish according to proper food-handling standards. *General rules for safe handling of meat and fish products were discussed in Chapter 1.* Another factor to consider is how long you plan to store your meat or fish in the freezer. Larger cuts of meat, like roasts, steaks, or whole poultry products such as a turkey, can be safely stored in the freezer for up to 12 months. Items like ground beef and some fatty fish products are only safe in the freezer for around three months. Fatty fish such as salmon, tuna, sardines, mackerel, and trout should not be stored in the freezer beyond three months. Meat and fish left in the freezer beyond recommended safe storage limits will have a deteriorated taste and will lose the natural tenderness you expect. Pork sausage should not be stored for more than two months. In any case, we are not talking about years and years of storage in your freezer. The following list provides a quick list of safe meat storage limits. Meat and fish products that have reached the end of the safe storage life in the freezer must be immediately cooked and consumed or properly disposed of.

GENERAL SAFE MEAT AND FISH STORAGE LIMITS

- Large items such as beef and lamb roasts ....12 months
- Lean fish, duck, and goose..6 months
- Fatty fish and ground meats ....3 months
- Pork chops ....4 months
- Light items such as bacon...1 month

The University of Georgia Cooperative Extension Service has a Web page titled "Preserving Food: Freezing Animal Products" that provides a detailed chart of proper time limits for leaving meat and fish in the freezer. *The Internet address for this Web page is listed in the Appendix.*

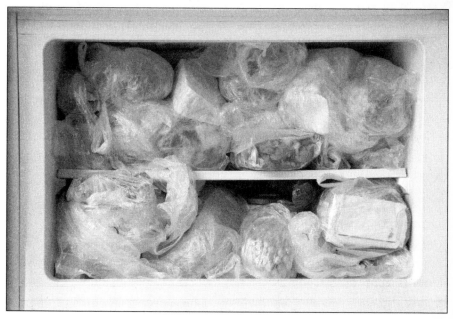

*A well-stocked freezer will make it easy
to figure out what is for dinner.*

After the freezer, the rest of the equipment you will need is much smaller by comparison. Good kitchen knives are essential tools for people who are preparing meat for storage or for cooking. Kitchen knives should be kept sharp to avoid wasting valuable meat products and to keep you from injuries that are caused by using dull knives. The dangers that go with using dull knives cannot be understated. Dull knives only tear meat products, which leads to waste and makes the meat difficult to cook because the torn edges will not heat uniformly with the rest of the cut of meat. Dull knives can also be dangerous to the user because of the force that is needed to saw through meat products. The best kitchen investment any family can make is to purchase the best quality knives the budget will allow. Modern knives that are made of high-carbon stainless steel are considered the best choice. Carbon steel is soft enough to respond well to sharpening, but has the strength of stainless steel. Two quality knife companies are Zwilling J.A. Henckels® and Wusthof®, both of Germany. Regardless of which company you choose to purchase knives from, make sure you select knives that you would expect to use for a lifetime. Many people are now turning to the new ceramic knives as the best choice. The best approach to take when the time comes to make a significant investment in knives is to do some research on your own. If you purchase knives from an established company that provides a good warranty, you probably will not regret the decision. *There are sources for good quality knives referenced in the Appendix to help you get started in your search.*

Using good quality cooking pots and skillets ensures that meat is thoroughly cooked without burning or scorching. Buying brand-new equipment does not mean you will have the best quality possible. If you look in your grandmother's kitchen cupboards, you will probably find some well-used equipment that will do a better job than a lot of the new stuff that is on the market today. For example, your grandmother may have some old-fashioned, high carbon steel knives in the drawer that will sharpen to a very fine cutting edge and yet remain very flexible. The only drawback to these knives is that they require extra care to keep them from tarnishing. Cooking pots and skillets that have been in use for many years and are still in good shape will continue to serve very well if you continue to take good care of them.

If you are going to grind meat to make hamburger of deer sausage, you will need as good of a grinder as your budget will allow. There are several items to consider when selecting a grinder for home use. The following short chart lists some important features to look for. *Sources for grinders have been included in the Appendix.*

- Can you get by with a hand-crank meat grinder, or do you need an electric grinder? This is important as you consider the volume of meat product that will be processed each year. There is not a specific recommendation for the amount of meat that would justify an upgrade to an electric grinder. If you will only use your grinder occasionally for small amounts of meat, then you may do very well with a manual machine. If you will use the machine on a regular basis, then the time and effort an electric machine will save may be sufficient to justify the extra expense of an electric machine. If you decide you need an electric model, then you must consider whether the power rating of the grinder is sufficient. You may be able to get along with a 150-watt machine that will handle most non-commercial kitchen meat grinding chores, or you may need a 1000-watt machine that is capable of grinding up to 175 pounds of meat in an hour. Purchasing a machine rated a little higher than you expect to need should ensure that you can meet any projected meat grinding chores that you may encounter throughout the life of your machine.

- Grinders that use stainless steel grinding and cutting blades will provide easier cleaning with an expectation of a longer useful service life than blades that are not made of high-quality stainless steel. Stainless steel blades may last up to three times longer than carbon steel blades because the carbon steel blades are more susceptible to corrosion and will not keep a sharp edge as long.

- Does the grinder include a food-pushing tool? A food-pushing tool provides the user with an extra measure of safety since the machine keeps fingers away from grinding blades.

- Is the rated capacity sufficient for the size of grinding projects you expect to accomplish?

- What is the durability rating of the grinder; does it have a good warranty?

To prepare your product for freezing, you will need freezer or butcher paper to wrap the meat or fish in. Some items, such as pork chops and ground beef patties, store better and separate easier when they are separated by freezer paper. There are a wide variety of plastic freezer containers you can use. Freezer bags are different than sandwich bags. Freezer bags are made of thicker material than sandwich bags, and they are manufactured with sealing features that are specifically designed to keep out air and moisture during long-term storage of food products. Sandwich bags will not provide the protection that frozen meats will need for long-term storage. Freezer storage bags come in many sizes. The key is to ensure that you use storage containers that have been made expressly for containing frozen food. Frozen food that will be consumed in small quantities should only be put in smaller bags, as it will be easier to close up the bag with the least amount of air left in the bag. Air and moisture that are allowed to remain in the bag will lead to freezer burn. Vacuum-sealing systems pull the air and moisture out of the freezer bag, and heat seals the bag securely.

An additional concern that needs to be addressed is how to keep track of what each freezer bag or container contains, and how long it has been in the freezer. Losing track of how long meat has been stored in the freezer will lead to waste. To solve this problem, you will need freezer labels to indicate what is in each container and the date it should be consumed by. A well-organized freezer will ensure that everything that has been prepared and stored will be available to feed your family and nothing will be lost. *A number of good resources for storing food have been listed in the Appendix.*

Farmers Bill and Kay Tomaszewski, along with their children, are very involved in preserving meat and fish in their home. With their extensive experience preserving meat, they provided another idea that would be helpful for people trying to preserve meat and fish in the home environment. "The ideal place to process meat is in a walk-in cooler to keep the meat cool to prevent deterioration and spoilage," Bill said. "We don't have that, but in the past we have processed in an outside room in the cold of winter. We process inside now — arthritis and age played a part in that — so we make sure everything is kept cool. The meat is maintained between 34 to 38 degrees. The room is kept less than 70 degrees Fahrenheit."

CASE STUDY: HARVESTING ICE FOR THE YEAR

Helen Ibsen Pyell
Westminster, Colorado
Member of Pioneer Family

Helen Ibsen Pyell remembers when she was a 12-year-old girl in rural Nebraska and how hard she and her family had to work to make a living on the family homestead. In the 1930s, electricity had not yet reached rural Nebraska. In the cold winter months, the men from each of the families in the area would take their wagons down to the Republican River and cut ice to provide natural refrigeration for their homes. Properly stored ice would provide natural refrigeration for many months. Pyell remembers that her father would lay straw on the bed of the wagon before he went down to the river. The men would use axes and hand tools to cut out 18- by 18-inch ice blocks and use ice tongs to manually lift them up into the wagon beds. This was a very difficult job to accomplish out in the freezing weather.

Pyell's family had a lean-to for an icehouse built against the northwest corner of the house so the sun would not shine directly on it during the daytime hours. The ice blocks would be stacked in the shed and packed with straw to insulate them against melting. Once the ice blocks were packed into the icehouse, they would last for several months. Pyell remembers a neighbor that had an icehouse built into the ground that kept ice all the way through the summer. The log cabin that she and her family lived in had a little door that opened into the ice shed. Every day they would reach into the ice storage and chip off enough ice to meet the needs of the day. With the ice, they had cooling for dairy products and fresh meat.

Pyell remembers making homemade ice cream using the ice from the ice shed. When it came time to make ice cream on a hot summer day, they would reach into the shed through the little door, which she fondly remembers as the "cubby hole," and pull out a chunk of ice. She or another member of the family would put the chunk of ice in a burlap sack and use a hammer to break the ice into small chips that would be packed around the sides of the hand-cranked ice cream machine. The ice from the cold winter months provided a wonderful treat for a little girl and her family on a farm far from the big city. Pyell remembers those years of hard work fondly, but she was very happy when electricity and refrigeration finally reached the homestead near Orleans, Nebraska.

Temperature requirements to fully cook meats

The finished cooking temperature of meat in restaurants has been much in the news the last few years. Many people like a good steak just a little on the "rare" side. The problem is that if the internal temperature is not high enough to kill dangerous bacteria, people can get very sick. The best way to ensure that the meat and fish you are preparing has been cooked enough is to use a meat thermometer. Satisfactory meat thermometers are not very expensive and can be easily obtained in the nearest hardware or department store.

General safe meat internal cooking temperatures
- Ground beef as in patties and meatloaf...........................160° F
- Ground poultry...165° F
- Well-done beef roast...170° F
- Well-done pork ....170° F

The important point to remember is that meat must be cooked sufficiently to destroy bacterium that would cause a foodborne disease. *A complete meat temperature chart from the University of Illinois is provided in the Appendix.*

CANNING EQUIPMENT AND SUPPLIES

An essential piece of equipment for the home canner is the pressure canner, also called a canning pressure cooker. A canning pressure cooker heats both the meat and the jars to sufficient temperature to ensure safe and sanitary preparation of the product. Meat being canned must be heated to 240 degrees to ensure the canning jars seal and the product remains safe for consumption for as long as possible. Simply boiling the product and the jars on the stove top will only bring the heat to 212 degrees, which is 28 degrees below the safe temperature level.

A pressure cooker works on the same principle as the radiator in a car does. In order to raise the temperature of water above the boiling point without the water turning to steam, water must be heated in a sealed container under pressure. The pressure cap on a radiator, depending on the application, holds between 13 to 15 pounds of pressure before it vents off some of that pressure. Pressure must be vented off to keep the radiator or some other cooling system component from exploding. The pressure on the radiator allows the cooling system to handle temperatures much higher than the boiling point, keeping your car engine from boiling over on hot days.

A pressure cooker designed for canning will have a lid that seals tightly with a pressure gauge and a vent. It is very important to follow the manufacturer's instructions for your elevation. Water boils at different temperatures according to elevation, so there will be different pressure requirements between coastal Florida and mile-high Colorado. Always inspect the seal and sealing mechanism for the lid whether the cooker is new or used. A lid that loses its seal after the pressure has built up is a formula for disaster. If a canning lid looses its seal, air can get into the meat, allowing deadly organisms such as botulism to grow that can cause food poisoning. People who become infected with a severe case of botulism can die from respiratory failure. People who receive timely medical treatment may have a long hospital stay requiring the use of a breathing machine with a long-term stay in an intensive care facility. Make sure the vent cap is working properly, and watch the gauge as the heat and pressure build. If there is a doubt that any part of the pressure canner is working correctly, remove the heat and fix the problem immediately.

A 16-quart pressure canner will help you make delicious canned meals, such as marinara sauce.

Pressure canner safety checklist

1. Check the rubber seal that goes around the lid to be sure it is not cracked or torn. If the seal is defective, do not use the pressure canner until a new seal is installed. Also inspect the seal for cleanliness. A lid with a dirty seal will not hold pressure properly.

2. The pressure gauge and pressure vent should be inspected for condition. If they are defective or not working properly, they must be replaced before using the pressure canner. A defective pressure gauge may have broken glass over the gauge, or the needle may be stuck. The pressure vent may be bent or deformed from other kitchen

equipment that was dropped on it in the cupboard, or it may have been damaged so it no longer sits on the lid properly any more.

3.   If the pressure is not building as it should or begins to drop, increase the cooking heat immediately.

4.   If the pressure drops below the prescribed amount on the chart for your pressure canner, increase the cooking heat to bring the pressure back up to specification. If this happens, you will need to begin the timing process all over again.

5.   If you live above 1,000 feet, you must adjust the pressure for elevation. A time and pressure adjustment chart is provided in the following case study.

6.   When the pressure canning process begins, all the trapped air must be vented out of the cooker. Air that remains in the canner will reduce the temperature that can be reached for a particular pressure. Most pressure canners require 10 minutes of venting to insure all of the excess air is vented from the interior of the canner. During venting, you will be able to see the air venting out in the form of steam. After 10 minutes of continuous steam vapor, close the vent and begin building up the pressure.

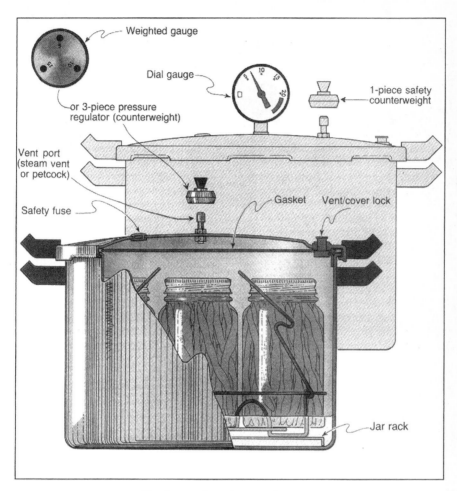

*This diagram shows the parts of a pressure
canner. Image courtesy of the USDA.*

CASE STUDY

David G. Blackburn
www.CanningUSA.com

David Blackburn has a very useful Web site on canning food, which includes a chart for adjusting canning cooking time and pressure adjustment for elevation. Blackburn allowed this chart from the Web site to be included in this book.

Water boils when its vapor pressure exceeds the atmospheric pressure, which reduces as the altitude increases. Water will boil and maintain a lower temperature at higher altitudes than at sea level. These lower boiling point temperatures increase the cooking times for any food, they increase the processing time for canning in a water bath, and they increase the pressure required to process in a pressure canner.

The temperatures and processing times that are listed in this chart are for elevations of sea level up to 1,000 feet. These adjustments should be made to ensure that your meat products are processed at a safe temperature and pressure for the elevation you live at.

Elevation, Time, and Pressure Canning Pressure Adjustment Chart

BOILING WATER TEMPERATURE CHART IN FAHRENHEIT

Sea Level	1,000 ft.	3,000 ft.	6,000 ft.	8,000 ft.
212°	210.1°	206.3°	200.6°	196.8°

(Reflects a 1.9° reduction for each 1,000 foot elevation increase)

WATER BATH CANNER PROCESSING TIMES IN MINUTES

Sea Level	1,000 ft.	3,000 ft.	6,000 ft.	8,000 ft.
5	10	15	20	25
10	15	20	25	30
15	20	25	30	35
30	35	40	45	50

Sea Level	1,000 ft.	3,000 ft.	6,000 ft.	8,000 ft.
45	50	55	60	65
60	65	70	75	80
75	80	85	90	95
90	95	100	110	120

ADJUSTMENT FOR PRESSURE CANNER, DIAL GAUGE

Sea Level	1,000 ft.	3,000 ft.	6,000 ft.	8,000 ft.
5 lbs.	6 lbs.	7 lbs.	8 lbs.	9 lbs.
10 lbs.	11.5 lbs.	13 lbs.	14 lbs.	15 lbs.

ADJUSTMENT FOR PRESSURE CANNER, WEIGHTED GAUGE

Sea Level	1,000 ft.	3,000 ft.	6,000 ft.	8,000 ft.
5 lbs.	10 lbs.	10 lbs.	10 lbs.	10 lbs.
11 lbs.	15 lbs.	15 lbs.	15 lbs.	15 lbs.

Processing times remain unchanged

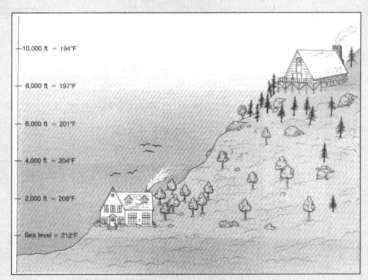

Be sure to research your altitude above sea level. Your local extension office should be able to tell your specifics about your area. Image courtesy of the USDA.

The key to ensuring that all jars are thoroughly heated is to be sure that no jars touch the sides of the pressure cooker and that no jars are touching each other. The hot water must be able to circulate completely around the canning jars to ensure that the meat and jars are completely brought up to the correct heat all the way through the contents of the jar. A jar that is touching the side of the pressure cooker or another jar may develop a "cold" spot. Canning jars should be left in the pressure canner after the removal of heat until the pressure returns to zero without any artificial cooling. The period of time the jars are left in the pressure canner after the heat has been removed is part of the processing time, and it is essential to finish the destruction of any deadly microorganisms. Do not rush the pressuring-down period by applying cool water or by using a cooling fan. The jars should be removed from the pressure canner just as soon as the pressure reaches zero. Set the jars on the counter to cool at room temperature. Jars with cold spots that have not been heated sufficiently will be easy to see after you set them on the counter to wait for the distinctive "pop" that indicates the jar has sealed properly. Meat that has not been cooked to a proper temperature will look differently than the meat in jars that has been heated properly. Canning jars should seal within 12 to 24 hours. Jars of meat that do not seal up properly must be refrigerated and consumed soon after or put back in the cooker to restart the process.

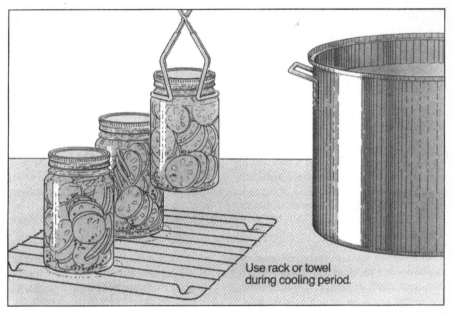

Use rack or towel during cooling period.

Cooling is an important part of the canning process. A rack and towel are all you need for cooling. Image courtesy of the USDA.

Always purchase the best canning pressure cooker you can afford. If you consider purchasing a used cooker, do a thorough inspection before the purchase is finalized. Check used pressure canners for cracks or deformities in the main body and the lid. Inspect the seal around the lid for cracks and stretching. Also inspect the pressure gauge for broken glass or a stuck needle. If the canner has a pressure vent, make sure it has not been damaged or bent. The safety of every person who eats the meat processed in the pressure cooker is at stake. There should never be any temptation to take shortcuts when canning meat or fish at any time for any reason.

The next question that many people ask is whether or not they can use a standard pressure cooker as a pressure canner. The answer is no. The standard pressure cooker uses less metal in its construction, and it is much smaller than a pressure canner. Since there is less metal in the standard pressure cooker, heating and cooling times will not be the same as a pressure canner. The total processing times in meat and fish canning recipes are based on the use of a pressure canner. If the meat or fish is under-processed, deadly organisms can form quickly, putting your family in danger of food poisoning.

A true pressure canner will include a wire rack for holding canning jars and will be able to hold at least four 1-quart jars. The wire rack allows hot water to circulate under the jars during cooking, and the pressure canner must be large enough so that hot water can completely circulate around the sides and top of the canning jars to ensure every part of the meat product is raised to a heat level sufficient to cook the meat and destroy any dangerous organisms. Finally, do not be tempted to create your own canning recipes. Established canning processing times have been developed by the United States Department of Agriculture (USDA) and are built into canning recipes. Canning meat and fish is not the place to be using your imagination. Please follow established canning recipes and procedures to ensure the safety of your loved ones. *Resources for pressure canners can be found in the Appendix.*

Canning jars are the most important ingredient in the recipe for a great day of canning. People have tried unsuccessfully to use pickle and jelly jars from the grocery store after they had been emptied. These types of jars are not made to withstand the temperatures and pressures of the canning pressure cooker. These types of jars expose you and your family to the danger of a jar bursting and causing a serious injury. Even genuine canning jars that have been in the family for a number of years may pose a risk of breakage or leakage. It is incumbent upon the person doing the canning to thoroughly inspect old jars for cracks in the body, chips around the top edge, or some weakness in the spiral grooves that will secure the lid.

There are four brand names of canning jars available in North America: Ball®, Kerr®, Bernardin®, and Golden Harvest®. Ball and Kerr jars use interchangeable lids and are considered to be of equal quality. Ball and Kerr canning jars can be found in most hardware and department stores around the country, although selection will be much better during the traditional fall canning season. Golden Harvest jars are sold in major discount department stores or hardware chain stores. Golden Harvest canning jars can be found at a lower price and have received mixed reviews, but they can serve very well if used with proper care. Bernardin canning jars are sold in Canada. Since 1993, all four brands have been made by the same company, Jarden Home Brands, which is a subsidiary of Jarden Corporation.

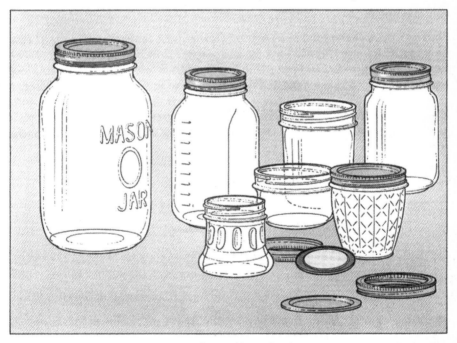

*Jars come in many shapes and sizes, but for meat, you
will use mostly quart jars. Image courtesy of the USDA.*

When selecting jars to can meat and fish, make sure you select jars that are large enough for the product that will be preserved. When the meat product is put in the jar, enough room must be left between the lid and the product for the canning sealing action to be successful. The amount of headspace you leave depends on the recipe and the product being canned, but it will generally be from ¼-inch to 1 inch. If you are using a recognized recipe, it will provide you with the specific headspace that will be required to safely can your food product. If a canning jar is filled too much, the product may boil out over the lip of the jar and make it impossible to get a good seal. Most meat and fish canning will be done with quart jars. *Internet Web page addresses for canning jar resources are listed in the Appendix.*

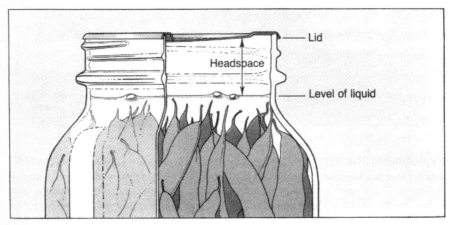

Proper headspace is essential to a good seal. Image courtesy of the USDA.

Proper care and sanitation of canning jars

By the very nature of being glass, canning jars can be easily broken. Children may be allowed to play with the pots and pans in the kitchen or may be allowed to rearrange the canned goods in the cupboard, but canning jars make dangerous toys.

With careful handling, canning jars can be used for many years. However, even the slightest crack or chip around the lid is sufficient reason to throw a jar out and get a new one. Some people may consider using the lids over, but that is not a recommended practice. The lids are generally bent or the sealing surface damaged when the jar was last opened. The metal rings that hold the lid down before being vacuum-sealed can be cleaned and used over again until they become distorted in some way.

Jars do not need to be sanitized separately when working with meat or fish because the sanitation process will take place in the pressure cooker. This is why the admonition in the last section was so strong to ensure the cooker gets to the correct heat and pressure for the elevation at which the canning is taking place. The success of a meat-canning project depends completely on getting enough heat around the jars to fully cook the meat, sanitize the jar and the contents, and get the vacuum seal to "pop."

After the jars of beautiful food are on the shelf, please do not get complacent. The jars can be jostled around and get cracked. Even the slightest crack will break the vacuum seal and allow air to get into the jar and start the spoilage process. Occasionally inspect stored jars of food for lids with seals that have broken loose. Lids can come unsealed for any number of reasons. For example, if the headspace was not correct, the vacuum that holds the seal may fail, or if the lip of the jar was contaminated with food juices when the jar was sealed, the seal may fail. If the seal is broken, the safe rule is to dispose of the jar's contents immediately as spoilage can take place rather quickly. During your inspection, if the food in a jar is a significantly different color than other jars with like product, it is a good indication that spoilage has taken place.

Quality canning jar lids are essential to the canning process. Canning jar lids include the round lid that fits on the top lip of the jar, and the outer band that secures the lid until the vacuum in the jar securely seals the lid. The outer bands hold the lid in place until the vacuum in the jar seals the lid. The vacuum seal takes place while the food is cooling over a 12- to 24-hour period. Once the lid is sealed, the bands are no longer necessary. Many people remove the bands at this point because the bands can rust in place and be difficult to remove later when you are ready to consume the meat.

Using flawless lids ensures a good seal.
Image courtesy of the USDA.

CURING AND DRYING EQUIPMENT, SUPPLIES, AND PROCEDURES

To understand the equipment that will be needed to cure and dry meat and fish, there is a need to understand the relationship between curing and drying. Curing is a process that uses an agent such as salt to preserve meat or fish for future use. The curing process is also used to impart a desired flavoring to meat or fish. It is important to remember that curing does not cook the meat, but rather preserves it for future use. Curing stops the biological processes that produce spoilage and cause harmful diseases.

Salt is the primary agent for meat curing in the home, but in some cases, nitrates can be used. Meat and fish are not usually cooked prior to the curing process.

Learning how to cure meat is a skill that anyone can master with some education and practice. Ideally, the best time to begin a meat-curing project is during the fall and winter months when the outside is cool or even cold. If you are curing meat during warm weather and you do not have a cooler or refrigerator large enough to hold all of your meat in one piece, then you will need to cut your meat into pieces that can be stored safely in your refrigerator. If you are really going to get involved in curing meat, a good investment would be an extra refrigerator that you could dedicate to these kinds of projects.

There are several procedures that fall under the title of meat curing. Meat can be cured in a brine solution made up of salt, water, saltpeter, and nitrite. Meat can be dry cured by rubbing a dry cure compound on the meat and packing the product into a cure box for a period of time. Sugar curing involves adding sugar to the cure formula. The sugar offsets the salt and imparts its own flavoring to the meat. Many people will use the word "curing" in conjunction with the use of smoke to impart flavor to meat and to cook it if the temperature in the smokehouse is allowed to get high enough. In all of these curing processes, the control of the temperature that the meat is being exposed to is the important factor. Before the meat has been cooked or cured, it must be kept cold. During the time that you are cutting or grinding the meat, it is important to keep the temperature as cold as possible to inhibit the growth of deadly microorganisms. Even after the meat has been cured, the shelf life of the product will be extended if it is kept under refrigeration.

In many procedures, it will be essential to keep the meat cool after it has been cured for several hours or even days to give the salt a chance to penetrate all the way through the cut of meat. If any step in the curing process is skipped or bypassed, your meat may be spoiled. Brine or dry cure processes are designed to allow salt to penetrate into the meat and dissolve or remove as much moisture as possible. The removal of moisture helps to inhibit the growth of bacteria. In this way, salt brings about the curing in the meat product.

Saltpeter is used to maintain the red or pink color in processed meats. Several manufacturers produce pre-mixed curing formulas that can be purchased in a number of sizes. Using a commercially prepared curing mixture takes much of the guesswork out of curing meat. The use of a commercially manufactured curing mixture will help you to eliminate errors. Sources for pre-mixed curing compounds are the local grocery store and the local butcher shop, or you can look on the Internet for reliable sources.

To ensure success when applying a sugar cure, simply remember to keep the meat cold throughout the entire curing process. Limit as much as possible the amount of time your uncured meat product is not at 38 to 40 degrees Fahrenheit. During the time the meat is exposed to the sugar cure, if the temperature gets too cold, it will interfere with penetration of the curing agents. If the temperature is allowed to rise above 40 degrees Fahrenheit, the spoilage processes will begin.

Always weigh and measure your ingredients exactly as the instructions require. There are several types of salt that may be used. Just remember that each type of salt will measure out differently, and each type of salt will have its own curing characteristics. A general recommendation is to use salt that has not been iodized. Always use the exact measurements as much as possible.

When you are waiting for a meat project to cure, remember that curing is not a job you can spend a few minutes on and it is done. Sufficient time must be allowed for the curing agent to be absorbed into the meat. If you try to cut short the time the meat is exposed to the curing agent, the meat will probably spoil long before you expect it to. If you leave the meat in the curing agent for too long, the meat will become extremely salty and not taste good.

This cured red pepperoni will make a delicious addition to a tray of cheese and crackers.

Dry curing involves rubbing a cure mixture on the surface of meat and packing it in a cure box for a period of time to allow the cure to naturally soak in and penetrate the meat completely. People have different approaches for rubbing the cure on the surface of the meat. Some people lightly rub the cure on the surface, making sure that all parts of the meat are covered. Other recipes direct you to rub the meat a number of times over a period of time. The best policy is to follow the instructions that are part of the recipe or procedure you are using. After you have become experienced in the art of preserving meat, you can experiment a little and find out what works best for you.

After you have rubbed your meat sufficiently, it is to be packed in a dry curing box. A dry curing box will have a bottom shelf with holes in it so that the brine that is produced can drain away from the meat. The meat will be loosely packed in layers with the dry cure compound packed all around each piece of meat. The curing box should be something that will not be reactive to the salt in the cure mixture, such as a wooden barrel, stoneware container, or even a burlap bag. The curing container is then put in a refrigerator set at the correct temperature, or if the weather is cool enough, out on the porch. Different recipes require that the rub be repeated periodically and the meat be turned over in the dry cure box. The frequency will be determined by the size of the meat cuts being cured, the amount of brine that is collecting in the bottom of the box, and the individual preference of the person curing the meat. It is not inconceivable that you will need to rotate the meat in the box every two or three days until the cure is complete. The entire process may take up to a week to complete.

When the curing cycle is complete, remove the meat from the curing pack and brush off the excess cure on the meat. You will then rinse all of the salt from the outside of the meat with cool clean water. This should not be done in a place where the runoff salt brine can damage a floor or counter top. This is the time to begin smoking the meat. The meat will need to be completely dry before it is exposed to the smoke and cooking process. Excess moisture on the meat works to counteract the effects of smoking.

The meat should be hung or placed on shelves in the smokehouse so that the pieces do not touch another piece of meat. Fire up the smokehouse using the type of hardwood that will impart the specific smoke flavor you are looking for. *A chart explaining the flavor that can be expected from different types of wood is provided in Chapter 1.* Some experienced smokers say that sawdust provides the best smoke, while others say to use small chunks of wood. If you have purchased a smoker in the store, follow the instructions that came with your smoker. Usually, cold or hot smoking takes more than one day to complete, so be patient.

Remember that cold smoking does not cook the meat. Cold-smoked meat will need to be cooked properly before it is consumed. Although hot smoking cooks the meat, it has been exposed to a curing agent, so it must still be refrigerated to extend the safe storage life of the meat. Never take any chances when it comes to food safety.

Drying meat and fish is the process of removing moisture, which aids in inhibiting the growth of bacteria. The main product that comes to mind when we think about drying is jerky. Making jerky is not a complicated process, but it provides a good example for learning the basics of drying meat. Only lean meats such as beef, deer, elk, or turkey are suitable for making jerky. Pork is sometimes too fatty to dry. During the drying process, the fatty portions are subject to oxidation and will turn rancid and stink, making the jerky inedible.

The relationship between curing and drying is important because meat and fish can be cured before they are exposed to the drying process, ensuring the product does not spoil before it is fully dried. Additionally, your desired flavoring can be added to the meat through the curing process. Meat that is going to be dried should be simmered or baked so it will be safe for consumption when it comes out of the dryer. Drying inhibits bacterial growth, but it does not destroy the organisms that cause disease. *There are sources for food dehydrators listed in the Appendix.* The following list describes the features you should look for in a food dehydrator:

- Stainless steel construction to increase durability and facilitate cleaning. A key to providing quality dried foods for your family is the ability to keep your machine clean. Plastic food driers may be subject to damage under hard use and may not be as easy to clean.

- The dehydrator you select should have the maximum possible space for everything you want to process in each session.

- The dehydrator you select should allow you to control the removal of moisture from the meat through the airflow. You do not want the meat to become hard and brittle when the drying process is complete, but sufficient moisture must be removed to prevent it from turning rancid. The controls should be easy to understand and operate.

- Select a machine that allows you to remove the shelves to facilitate not only cleaning, but also the placement of your meat or fish product.

- Although a built-in timer is not essential since you can use an external timer, it may be a very convenient option for you.

- It is important to select the correct size dehydrator so that you do not have a machine that is significantly larger than your need, or a machine that is so small it does not handle the amount of meat or fish you wish to dry efficiently.

- Modern technology makes it possible to purchase a machine with built-in programming features to make the process much more efficient.

This assortment of dried, cured, and boiled
meat shows several preserving options.

The types and amount of equipment and supplies needed to cure meat depends completely on how large an operation you desire to have. People just beginning to learn how to cure meat can unnecessarily spend hundreds of dollars initially instead of slowly building up the equipment and supplies they will need. Many households already have plenty of utensils and supplies that can be adapted to use as curing equipment. For example, to cure with salt brine, a large plastic tub will suffice for mixing for the brine to cure the meat product. Meat and fish can be cut to size with kitchen knives that you already possess. Any cooking that will be required can be done in pots and pans that are already in the cupboard. If there is ready availability, the next step up is a large crock or hardwood barrel of sufficient size for the curing project you have in mind.

There are actually two primary methods used to dry cure meats and fish. In the first method, a dry cure compound is rubbed on the meat to start the preservation process. The dry cure compound will include salt, sodium nitrates, and the seasoning you desire to impart a particular flavor to the meat. After the curing compound is rubbed on the surface of the meat, the product is hung in a place that is dry, cool, and free from outside influences. A damp basement will not be a suitable place to hang meat to dry cure. The ideal dry curing temperature is between 38 degrees Fahrenheit to 40 degrees Fahrenheit. The meat hangs for periods of a few weeks to a year or more. The usual curing and drying time using this method is about six months. As the meat hangs, the cure will penetrate the meat at the same time the moisture content of the meat is reduced. When the time comes to bring the meat in, the weight will be reduced due to the loss of moisture. The long curing time will impart an intense flavor to the meat along with a darker coloring. This method is used to produce dry cured hams.

The second dry cure method involves using a container and actually packing the meat in the curing compound. There are a many variations in the methods people use to dry pack or dry cure meat and fish, but the basic principles are all the same. Before the meat is packed in the curing compound, the surface of the meat or fish should be rubbed with it. Regardless of the exact dry pack container you have, make sure it is large enough to hold the meat cuts and the dry pack compound. Place a layer of salt cure compound on the bottom of the curing surface. The curing surface should be supported above the bottom of the curing box since a brine mixture will form below the meat as moisture is drawn out of the meat and mixes with the salt. If a wooden box is used, then holes can be cut in the bottom for the liquid to drain out.

Place the meat on the bottom salt layer and cover the meat completely with the curing mixture. If more than one piece of meat will be cured, be sure they do not touch each other. Meat such as pork cuts, for example, can be stacked as long as there is a layer of salt between each piece of meat.

One curing process requires that the procedure for placing the meat in the curing box should be repeated every two days for the first six days the meat is in the cure. In this process, each time the meat is repacked, the salt mixture should be completely changed and the old salt mixture disposed of. Another recipe suggests that the salt pack be changed every 12 hours for the first 24 hours. After a week in the dry cure pack, the meat is removed and can be stored under refrigeration or put through a smoking process. A key point to remember is that the danger zone for meat is between 40 and 140 degrees. Even meat that is thoroughly cured and smoked will not remain edible indefinitely.

A good question at this point would be what type of wood should the box be made of? There is not any particular type of wood that seems to be better for building a dry curing box. The exact design of the box is up to the builder as long as the box has a lid, holes in the bottom, is large enough for the meat and salt pack, and is supported off the ground. People have used old refrigerators, Styrofoam or plastic boxes, or even a burlap bag and hung the dry pack of meat from the rafters in a shed, as long as the temperature was cool enough. If the outside temperature is not cold enough, the meat will need to be hung in a refrigerator. A point to remember is that the salt in the cure will also have a long-term effect on your dry curing box. Salt can have a corrosive effect on metal and can deteriorate wood when in contact for long periods of time. Plastic will not be as adversely affected. It will be important to clean your dry cure box completely of salt when it is not in use.

The following case study provides two plans and should provide ample instruction on how to make both a dry cure cabinet to hang meat in, and how to make a box for packing meat in a dry cure mixture.

CASE STUDY: MAKING A DRY-CURING CHAMBER

Miroslaw Stanuszek
The Sausage Maker, Inc
www.sausagemaker.com

This case study has been included as an example of using ingenuity and creativity to find materials that have been cast aside to build a very useful meat-drying chamber. The plan that is outlined is adapted from the Sausage Maker Web site courtesy of Miroslaw Stanuszek.

When doing research into dry curing, I soon realized how precious little there is on the subject. The dry-curing method I am referring to is the hanging of sausages filled with choice meats, salt, dextrose (or sugar), fresh spices, or sodium nitrate in a controlled environment with relatively low temperatures and high humidity. Ideally, this is done where the climate has the best combination of temperature and humidity. This is why Italy has for so long produced the best dry-cured meat products, called "salumi," and for the same reason San Francisco has become the unofficial U.S. capital of Italian salumi. Do not confuse the word salumi with the meat product called salami. Salumi is a distinct style of preparing meat products usually based on pork. Some of the traditional dry-cured meats include: sopressata, capicola, prosciutto, pepperoni, and the leader of the pack, salami. Sopressata is Italian dry-cured salami, capicola is an Italian cold cut made from the shoulder or neck of a hog, and prosciutto is a salt-cured ham that is usually sliced very thin when served.

Most people live in climates and environments that do not have ideal temperatures and humidity for prolonged periods of time. So, we have to create them. Once the controlled space has been created, it will not matter where you live or what season it is. That was one of the main reasons for making this curing chamber; it will take the climate in your location virtually out of the equation by letting you create your own micro-climate.

The first step in the process is to find something that will provide hanging space and keep a cold temperature, like a refrigerator. It should be relatively easy for most people to find an old fridge on Craigslist

(***www.craigslist.org***) or in the classified section of the newspaper rang-
ing from $50 to $300. Picture number one shows the type of refrigerator
that will work here.

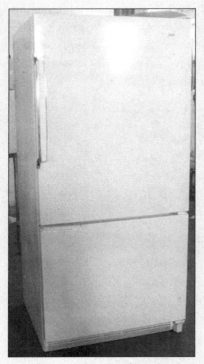

Picture 1: A basic refrigerator

The majority of refrigerators sold are "frost-free," but this will not be a problem because the automatic defrosting will be countered by the humidifier
and the humidity controller. The fridge we have has the freezer on the
bottom, which is a major plus for a chamber. Refrigerators that have the
freezer on the left or right side of the fridge provide less room for hanging
large diameter salami or prosciutto, so I would not recommend them as
highly. I would also strongly recommend you purchase a refrigerator with
a three-prong plug. On the electrical plug, the round prong is the electrical
ground. A grounded plug provides an extra measure of safety when the
refrigerator is being used. The ground prong protects you from electrical
shock when the appliance is plugged in or unplugged from the electrical
outlet on the wall.

The first step in preparing the refrigerator is to gut the fridge of all its loose shelves and lockers. Thoroughly clean it, and even if it appears clean, use an antibacterial cleaner with bleach. Make sure you clean all of the corners very thoroughly to ensure that any mold that may be hiding there is removed. The conditions for "bad" mold growth will be introduced into this relatively small space. We want the *good* mold to form on our products' casings, not the potentially dangerous foreign mold. Picture number two shows a thoroughly cleaned interior.

Picture 3: Temperature Controller

Picture 2: Properly cleaned refrigerator

At this point, test the refrigerator without the temperature controller to see what the lowest, or warmest, setting is. Ours was around 38 degrees Fahrenheit, which is too cold. We plugged the fridge into the temperature controller and set the temperature to 46 degrees. The fridge turned on once the temperature rose 2 degrees above 46 degrees. The cooling compressor kicked into gear and the temperature started to steadily drop. When it got to the set temperature, it turned off again. The cycle continues for as long as the batteries are working or the unit is plugged in. Picture number three shows the temperature controller in our refrigerator.

When buying a used refrigerator, there is little hope that the seller will still have the manual or diagrams that it may have come with originally; ours didn't either. The refrigerator we have had a light fixture in the precarious portion of the freezer where we wanted to cut a large hole, so this is what we did. Find the model number of the unit; we found ours on a plate/label on the ceiling of the fridge in plain view. The manufacturer's name is also on the label; jot it down and locate it from the list on Appliance411 (***www.appliance411.com***). When you enter the respective model's site, there should be a model number search. You should then be able to find schematics of the inner-workings of your unit — the parts, components, and location of wiring. Picture number four shows the label on this refrigerator.

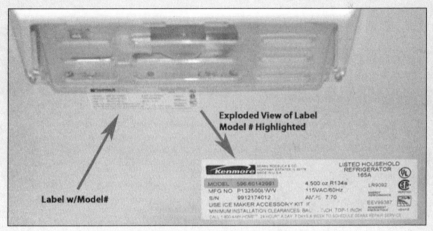

Picture 4: Label with model number

You have to be able to hang the meat from something. You can do it large smokehouse style, drill in some shelving brackets on the side walls, and when ready, hang the salami off of the resting wooden or metal dowels. Another option is strategically putting screw-hooks into the ceiling of the fridge and then hanging the products off the hooks; problems here would be the hooks' permanence and more likelihood of the product pulling the hooks out. But if done right, the screw hooks could be satisfactory. We decided on the brackets. Whatever you use, secure it well. With the amount of relative humidity and length of time per usage, you will want to use stainless steel screws, brackets, hooks, or ABS plastics.

Next, cut out a large opening in the fridge/freezer divider. This will provide more usable space. This section will be the new home of the humidifier. The sidewalls and door typically contain nothing more than insulation, but be very careful not to damage the cooling system, as it may have wiring. Picture number five shows our messy beginning.

Picture 5: The beginning cut to open up the refrigerator and freezer compartment. This picture shows the process of cutting a hole between the freezing and cooling compartment, which is very messy. The unit must be unplugged prior to cutting.

To cut the plastic interior refrigerator walls, simply use a box cutter to cut the plastic and a large knife for the insulation. The interior of the walls will be almost entirely insulation, so it will get everywhere when cutting. If you do accidentally cut the wires, which I did, splice and elongate them so you can hide them along the sides before covering the exposed areas. The electrical wires will be covered behind a protective shield so they are not exposed to the work you will do in your curing chamber. This can be covered with plastic wrap, hot-gluing plastic (ABS) strips over it, or forming stainless steel over and screwing it in. You can use any food-safe materials to simply cover the exposed area. We have a lot of scrap metals in our shop, so I used stainless steel and made it into large "C" brackets, locked them tightly into place with stainless steel screws, and filled in the cracks with food-grade silicone sealant. The hole we cut was large enough to allow free flow of mist out of our humidifier into the chamber. Pictures five and six clearly show this part of the process.

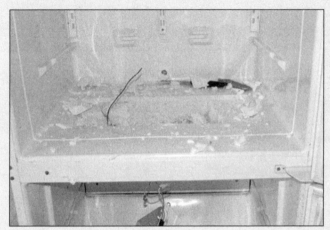

Picture 6: Cutting through the interior walls and insulation. This picture shows the vent.

It would have been a good idea to tape closed the back vent before we began cutting to keep residue from the plastic and insulations from falling down into the vent. Picture number seven shows the hole cut with the cutting mess removed and the wires exposed. Since we did not know which wires were necessary for the operation of the refrigerator, we lengthened them and made them ready to be tucked into the insulation; pictures seven and eight show this step very well.

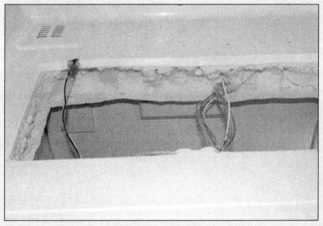

Picture 7: Wiring exposed (left)   Picture 8: Wiring extended (right)

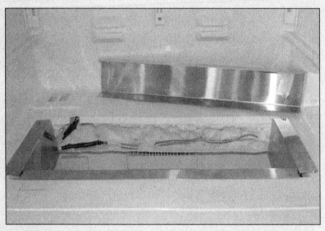

Picture 9: Wiring effectively extended and hidden along sides.

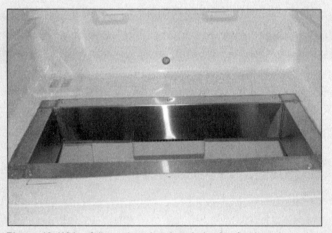

Picture 10: Wiring fully enclosed and sealed using food-grade sealant.

(1) Using a humidifier with a built-in hygrostat to maintain relative humidity in chamber. (2) An extra analog hygrometer. (3) Temperature controller. (4) Hygrometer to keep accurate readings of both humidity and temperature units.

1) Basic on/off and flow control humidifier. (2) Pair of 75-watt bulbs in moisture-proof holders for incubation stage. (3) Humidity controller (different in picture than available). (4) Extra analog hygrometer as backup. (5) Temperature controller. (6) Hygrometer.

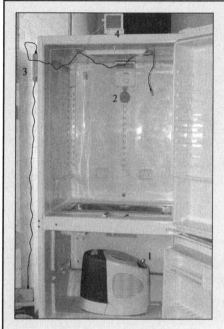
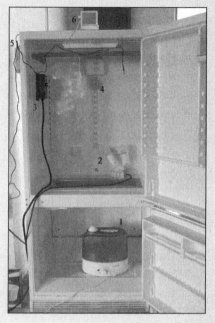

Without Humidity Controller *With Humidity Controller*

The aging/curing/fermenting chamber is completed. In *both* pictures above, the temperature controller is located on the top-left outside wall; it came with a bracket for installation. The controller will keep the internal temperature steady. The humidifier will produce moisture to the levels we need, but this would be more accurate with the humidity controller. Distilled water is highly recommended for the humidifier, as it does not have calcium and metals, plus it is easier on the filter and humidifier in general. I cut a notch in the refrigerator's gasket for the thick cables (cords) to pass through without breaking the door's seal, and the thin wires from the probes are simply pushed against the door's gasket when closed; moisture escaping through the tiny space it creates is insignificant. The hygrometer is on top of the unit, held in place with two simple homemade "L" brackets. The chamber is ready for use.

Now that the unit is complete, it is time for the test run. Test your chamber thoroughly with no meat at first, and document the results. What is the inside temperature's range? How about the humidity? Keep good records of the testing because they may come in handy later. There may have to be tweaks along the way, as it likely will not be perfect. Once you are satisfied, it is time to get it started with an actual recipe. You will notice that many dry-curing recipes demand a warm and moist environment to incubate for a couple hours or even days before they are put in a cool place. The temperatures in those recipes are unlikely to reach beyond 90 degrees Fahrenheit, so a hot plate may be overkill. We put two 75-watt incandescent light bulbs inside, not too close to the walls, and plugged them into the temperature controller, which we set to "heat" and set our high temperature. The bulbs were connected to outdoor weatherproof lamp holders to protect from exposure to the humidity, so we strongly recommend you use weatherproof holders and/or bulbs. Now that you have a chamber of your own, start with a less demanding recipe, such as pepperoni, before going into something like a large-diameter salami. The six-month or longer recipes for products like prosciutto or capicola may be difficult to duplicate with this relatively small unit. Do not try such demanding projects before becoming completely knowledgeable and experienced on the subject of dry curing.

BRINE CURING

The next process to explain is wet curing in liquid brine solutions. Brine curing of meat or fish is a process in which the product is soaked in a solution of salt for 24 to 48 hours. Brine solutions follow a number of different formulas depending on the type of meat or the length of time the meat is to be kept unrefrigerated. Suitable containers for soaking meat depend on the size of the cut of meat being salted. For small pieces of meat, a kitchen crock will do just fine. If you are going to use a brine solution to salt large quantities of meat, a large plastic tub or barrel that will hold water may be necessary.

Two other important tools for the curing process are a brine pump and a kitchen scale. The brine pump is used to inject the salt brine mixture into larger pieces of meat that may be too large for the salt brine to penetrate into. The kitchen scale is useful to know the weight of the meat product when mixing the salt brine or dry salt pack. Too much or too little salt will have significant impact on the success of the curing project. *Several good resources on curing can be found listed in the Appendix.*

Simple steps to make jerky:

- Slice meat into strips, cutting with the grain. The strips of meat should be ¼-inch thick. If the meat is slightly frozen, it may be easier to slice.

- To ensure the safety of the product for human consumption, the meat will need to be heated until the internal temperature reaches 160 degrees, either during the time it is soaking in the marinade or after it has been dried.

- If the meat is to be brought to an internal temperature of 160 degrees after it has finished drying, simply set the oven to 275 degrees, place the jerky on a flat baking pan, and heat the meat for about 10 minutes. If the strips are thicker than ¼-inch, it may take a little longer for the meat to reach the necessary internal temperature.

- The meat may be cooked by simmering it in marinade to flavor the meat to personal preference. *Recipes are provided throughout the book for the various types of meats that work well as jerky.*

- Remove the strips from the cooking liquid and drain. The strips may be placed in a preheated oven or dehydrator at around 170 degrees. Leave the oven door slightly ajar. This allows the moisture being removed from the meat to escape the oven. This process will take several hours. Any type of flavoring preferred can be spread on the jerky as the drying process is begun.

- The meat will shrivel up and turn a darker color as the moisture in the meat is removed.

- Remove the meat from the heat before it becomes too dry and hard to eat. The meat should be checked for tenderness after the first three hours of drying. The amount of time it will take to dry depends on the thickness of the strips and the type of meat that is being dried.

- Wipe off any remaining fat that has come to the surface.

- Jerky can be stored up to two months if dried properly, but will stay usable much longer if placed in a freezer bag and frozen. If jerky is kept in a refrigerator, or even frozen, it can be stored for up to a year.

Use your imagination when smoking meat and jerky. Any flavor combination can be added to the meat or fish. A fun way to experiment would be to try a variety of meat and fish. Simply look at all the different types of lean meat and fish that are covered in this book, and try something new and different. Using the kitchen oven the way it was described above may be a bit too expensive of a way to make jerky, as it will add significantly to your utility bill if you are going to prepare large amounts of meat. If you plan to get serious about making jerky, purchasing a good dehydrator would be a good investment. Dehydrators remove the moisture from food to preserve the product for storage and use at a later time. Removing moisture aids in inhibiting the growth of bacteria that can cause the food to spoil. Dehydrators have a heating element, a fan to circulate the air around the meat, and trays to lay the food on. To be successful, the drying process must bring the moisture content of the food product down to 15 percent or less. Food dehydrators are a very economical method for drying foods. *There is a good commercial resource for dehydrators listed in the Appendix.*

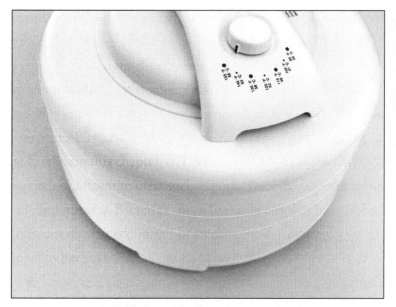

*Food dehydrators like this one can be purchased
at nearly any retailer that has home goods.*

SMOKERS AND SMOKING SUPPLIES

Smoking meat and fish may be the most popular way to preserve meat products. Smoked meat products come in a wide variety of styles and flavors. Many of the meat preparation procedures discussed already may also be considered preliminary steps to getting meat ready for the smoker. Smokers come in as many forms as there are people who use them. The common elements of a good smoker are a way to burn wood to make smoke, a chamber to hang the meat and expose the product to the smoke, a way to control the air flow, and a way to control the heat the meat is exposed to. The simplest homemade smoker can be made from a large metal garbage can, or you can create much more elaborate smokehouses made of brick. There are many commercially manufactured smokers available that use propane or electricity to produce heat to get the wood chips hot enough to make smoke.

With a little creativity, most people can find most of the necessary parts for a great smoker in the garage or lying around in the backyard. Some items that could be used in a smoker are racks to either hang or lay the meat on, pipe to transfer the smoke from the firebox to the smokehouse, or vents that could be used in the air flow system in the smokehouse. Here are a few ideas to start your creative juices flowing. Maybe you will have most of the necessary ingredients right in your backyard to build a wonderful smoker. The following list gives some ideas.

This homemade smoker preserves meat and
fish through a fumigation action.

Smoker ideas

- The box could be made from an old shed.

- The box could be made from an old refrigerator.

- The box could be made from a clean 55-gallon drum.

- An important thing to think about will be temperature control. When cold smoking, the temperature must not get above 100 degrees, and when hot smoking, the temperature must bring the meat to a high enough temperature to cook it, usually 160 degrees. *The case study by Bill Tomaszewski in Chapter 9 has an excellent discussion on smokehouse temperature control.*

- If an old refrigerator is used, the door needs to be secured so children and curious people are not able to get in and disrupt the controlled temperature. Also, dirt and moisture need to stay out.

- Other ideas include cutting a 55-gallon drum in half and using it to build a horizontal smoker, or you could go out and purchase a new commercially made smoker system. *There are some commercial smoker resources listed in the Appendix.*

There is also a picture of a good homemade smoker in Chapter 5 in the case study titled the "Tin Man Smokehouse." If you are not a person who can build a smoker, there are many commercially manufactured smokers on the market that will do a wonderful job. Smokers can be purchased in any size and within any budget constraints you have.

The other major concern is the type and availability of wood. Depending on locality, quality wood can become expensive. Places to look for scrap wood are carpenter shops, sawmills, lumberyards, and a firewood business that cuts hardwoods. Some practice will be required to find the correct balance between a hot-burning fire and being able to hold down the flame to make smoke. Good hot coals from hardwood may be made to smolder and smoke for a long time with a little practice. A good example is the modern wood-burning stove people use to heat their homes. By controlling the air that enters the firebox, a well-built-up bank of wood and coals can be made to produce heat all night long. The quality of the smoke produced has a direct relationship to the quality of smoked meat that comes out of the smoker at the end of the day.

Other pieces of equipment that will be needed are cooking utensils such as knives, spatulas, pots, and pans. Also, the meat will need to be refrigerated once the meat is through being smoked. A meat thermometer is also a very important tool to have. The length of time meat or fish should be left in the smoker will depend on the recipe, size of meat cuts, and how strong the desired smoke flavoring is expected to be. The following charts will provide some time and temperature specifications for hot smoking and cold smoking meat, fish, and game.

Sample hot smoking chart

Type of Meat	Temp during Smoking	Time to Expose to Smoke	Completed Temp
Brisket, sliced	225° F	1.5 hr/lb	180° F
Brisket, pulled	225° F	1.5 hr/lb	195° F
Beef Ribs	225° F	3 hr	175° F
Pork Butt, sliced	225° F	1.5 hr/lb	175° F
Pork Butt, pulled	225° F	1.5 hr/lb	190 to 205° F
Breakfast Sausage	230° F	3 hr	160° F
Spare Ribs	225 to 240° F	6 hr	172° F
Whole Chicken	250° F	4 hr	167° F
Chicken Thighs	250° F	1.5 hr	167° F

Chicken Quarters	250° F	3 hr	167° F
Whole Turkey 12 lb	240° F	5 to 6 hr	170° F
Turkey leg	250° F	4 hr	165° F
Turkey Wings	225° F	2.5 hr	165° F
Whole Duck	225 to 250°F	3 to 4 hr	170° F
Pheasant	200° F	2.5 to 3 hr	170° F
Rabbit, 3.5 lb	200° F	3.5 to 4 hr	160° F
Venison Roast	200 to 225° F	1 to 1.5 hr	160° F
Catfish	225 to 250° F	2 to 3 hr	Until Done

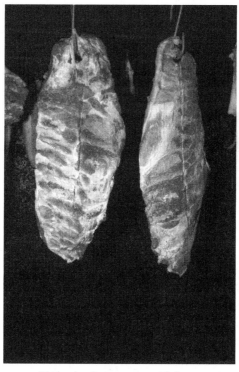

This pork is hanging in a smokehouse.

Cold smoking tips

1. The ideal cold smoking temperature is 70 degrees Fahrenheit to 80 degrees Fahrenheit.

2. The temperature in a cold smoking chamber should never be allowed to exceed 90 degrees Fahrenheit to 100 degrees Fahrenheit.

3. The best time to cold smoke meat and fish is during the cooler months so that the temperature around the cold smoker is not above 70 degrees Fahrenheit.

4. If the humidity is low, the smoking process will become more of a drying process than a smoking process. Ideally, you should smoke meat and fish when the humidity is around 70 percent.

5. Safe smoking depends on how strong of a curing formula the meat and fish were exposed to. If the meat only received a light cure, then the smoking time must be limited to a few hours to prevent spoilage. If the meat or fish received a heavy brining, then the smoking process can continue for a few days to a few weeks. The concern is the growth of bacteria, since cold smoking does not bring the meat to a safe cooking temperature. If you desire a deep smoked flavor that comes from extended time in the smoker, then the meat or fish must be exposed to a heavy brine mixture prior to smoking.

6. At the conclusion of the smoking process, if the product will not be cooked immediately, it must be refrigerated.

MEASUREMENTS TO HELP MAKE QUANTITY ADJUSTMENT IN RECIPES

Since many of the recipes in this book may be for quantities that are too large for you to conveniently use, this chart will help you to figure out how to reduce — or even increase — a recipe. Always remember the basics of required cooking temperatures; pressure canning times and pressure settings cannot be reduced. Some herbs and seasonings can change the flavor of a recipe very dramatically, so be careful when adding large quantities of herbs and seasonings.

Tables for Converting Ingredient Weights and Equivalent Measures

The information for this chart provided courtesy of North Dakota State University Extension and Julie Garden-Robinson.

Equivalent Measurements		
4 cups = 1 quart	2 pints = 1 quart	16 ounces = 1 pint
2 cups = 1 pint	2 cups = 16 fluid ounces	16 tablespoons = 1 cup
8 liquid ounces = 1 cup	4 tablespoons = ¼ cup	¼ cup = 2 liquid ounces
1 liquid ounce = 2 tablespoons	3 teaspoons = 1 tablespoon	1 pound salt = 1 ½ cups
1 pound sugar = 2 ¼ cups	1 ounce cure = 1 ½ tablespoons	1 ounce MSG = 2 ⅓ tablespoons

Approximate weights and measures of various spices

Conversion from ounces to tablespoons

Name of Spice	¼ ounce	½ ounce	¾ ounce	1 ounce	2 ounce	3 ounce	4 ounce
				to Tablespoons			
Allspice	1 ½	2 ½	3 ¾	5	10	15	20
Basil	1 ½	3	4 ½	6	12	18	24
Caraway	1 ¼	1 ¾	2 ⅗	3 ½	7	0 ½	14
Cardamom	1	2	3	4	8	12	16
Celery, ground	1	2	3	4	8	12	16
Cinnamon	⁹⁄₁₀	1 ¾	2 ⅔	3 ½	7	10 ½	14
Cloves, ground	1	2	3	4	8	12	16
Coriander, ground	1	2	3	4	8	12	16
Cumin	1	2	3	4	8	12	16
Dill, whole	1	2	3	3 ⁹⁄₁₀	7 ⅘	11 ⁷⁄₁₀	15
Fennel, whole	1	2 ¼	3 ⅓	4 ½	9	13 ½	18
Garlic powder	¾	1 ½	2 ¼	3	6	9	12
Ginger	1 ¼	2 ½	3 ¾	5	10	15	20
Mace, ground	1 ⅓	2 ¾	4	5 ½	11	16 ½	22
Marjoram	1 ½	3	4 ½	6	12	18	24
MSG	½	1	1 ⅓	2 ⅕	4 ⅖	6 ⅗	9
Mustard	1	2	3	4	8	12	16

Name of Spice	¼ ounce	½ ounce	¾ ounce	1 ounce	2 ounce	3 ounce	4 ounce
				to Tablespoons			
Nutmeg	1	2	3	4	8	12	16
Onion powder	1	2	3	4	8	12	16
Oregano	2	4	6	8	16	24	32
Paprika	1	2	3	4	8	12	16
Parsley flakes	3	6	12	16	32	48	64
Pepper, black	1	2	3	4	8	12	16
Pepper, ground	9/10	1 9/10	2 ¾	3 7/10	7 ⅖	11 1/10	15
Rosemary, ground	1 ¾	3 ½	5 ¼	7	14	21	28
Sage, ground	2 ½	3 ½	5	7 ½	14	21	28
Salt	½	1	1 ½	2	4	6	8
Savory	1 ⅓	2 ¾	4	5 ½	11	16 ½	22
Thyme	1 ¾	3 ½	5 ¼	7	14	21	28
Turmeric, ground	11/20	1 ¾	2 ⅔	3 ½	7	10 ½	14

CHAPTER 3:
How about Beef for Dinner Tonight?

European explorers brought cattle to North America in the early 1500s along with horses, sheep, and poultry. The vast grasslands of the North American interior proved to be an ideal place to raise vast numbers of cattle. Because of the ready availability of feed, and the need to feed a growing nation, beef grew to become the most consumed meat product in North America. The cattle industry has become one of the largest segments of agriculture in this country.

There is a rich American heritage that surrounds the cattle industry. After the Civil War, a way of life developed around the great cattle drives, and the influences of those times affect our culture even to this day. Although the actual cattle drive experience of the 19th century only lasted about 20 years, cowboys, the rodeo, and the importance of eating good beef are all still important to us in the 21st century.

This chapter will present information on additional food safety issues that are of importance to the preparation and consumption of beef and veal. Veal is the meat from beef calves that have been slaughtered at a very young age. Many consumers prefer the texture and flavor of the meat from young calves. A detailed description of currently available veal products is included in the next section of this chapter.

Some good recipes for cooking beef, and any special food preparation equipment that is particularly useful when preparing a good cut of beef, will be presented in this chapter. There is nothing better than a good cut of beef prepared on the grill after a hard day at work. One of the greatest blessings of our land is the opportunity we have to take time off from work, get away with our family, and put a good cut of meat on the grill. Understanding the best ways to safely preserve, prepare, and serve great food to our families is one way we can ensure that our wonderful American cultural heritage will be preserved for generations to come.

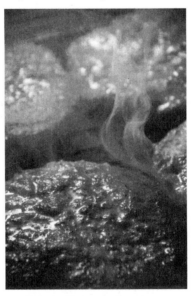

*These beef hamburgers smoking on
the grill are a cookout staple.*

DIFFERENCES IN BEEF AND VEAL

Many people have little experience with the properties of veal, so a little background knowledge on veal would be helpful before launching into the preservation of this quality meat. There are several categories of veal available on the retail market today. The following list provides information on the five types of veal that are available on the retail market.

Veal products

Bob veal: This type of veal comes from calves that are slaughtered when they are only a few days old. These are usually dairy calves. This product is only available in the United States. The meat is light pink in color with a soft texture.

Formula-fed veal: This type of veal comes from calves that are slaughtered when they are 18 to 20 weeks old. The meat is ivory or creamy pink in color with a firm and fine appearance.

Non-formula-fed veal: This type of veal comes from calves that are slaughtered when they are 22 to 26 weeks old. This product is sold as "calf meat" in retail outlets. These calves are fed grain and hay in addition to milk. The meat is a darker red in color with some marbling and fat.

Rose veal: This type of veal comes from calves that are slaughtered when they are 35 weeks old and is available in the United Kingdom. The meat is pink in color.

Free-raised veal: This type of veal comes from calves that are slaughtered when they are 24 weeks old. The calves are raised on their mother's milk and pasture grasses without the introduction of growth hormones or antibiotics. The meat is rich pink in color with a lower fat content than other types of veal.

There are significant differences in the way veal is best prepared and the usual preparation methods for beef. Since veal is lower in fat than beef, you must take care not to overcook the product and make it tough. This is important to the home meat preserver since the differences in the fat content and the finer texture of the meat will make cooking temperatures and cooking times different. The goal in preparing veal is to retain the smoother texture and taste you paid the higher price to get. Since veal is low in fat content, it would work well for drying and making jerky, although the premium price that is paid for the meat will make it expensive jerky. *If you need more information on the subject of veal, there is a resource in the Appendix that may be useful to you.*

Beef products

Good beef can come from a very wide range of sources. People who are going to get serious about this idea of preserving meat may want to take the time to consider the best source for good quality meat in their local communities. Homegrown beef without steroids or other chemical supplements is at a premium in the retail market. A good place to check for quality meat is at the local butcher or locker plant. Please get the best cut of meat for your project that your personal budget will allow. Taking shortcuts will only lead to disappointment. There are nine identified areas on a steer that produce the various cuts of beef people enjoy. The following chart identifies the nine areas of the steer and the beef products that come from each part of the animal.

Cuts of Beef Available on the Retail Market

Area of the Animal	Cut of Beef	Approximate Retail Price
Shoulder area	Chuck Arm Roast	$3.79 /lb
	Chuck Shoulder Pot Roast	$5.99 /lb
	Top Blade Steak	$5.99 /lb
	Chuck Steak	$5.15 /lb
Rib area	Prime Rib Roast	$28.99 /lb
	Ribeye Roast	$7.99 /lb
	Ribeye Steak	$9.95 /lb
	Rib Steak	$7.70 /lb
	Boneless Rib Steak	$12.79 /lb

Short Loin area	Tenderloin Roast	$8.99 /lb
	T-bone steak	$8.90 /lb
	Tenderloin Steak	$16.99 /lb
	Top Loin Steak, boneless	$4.49 /lb
Sirloin area	Tri-tip Roast	$5.29 /lb
	Sirloin Steak	$6.25 /lb
	Bottom Sirloin Steak	$6.45 /lb
Round area (rear leg)	Bottom Round Roast	$5.29 /lb
	Round Tip Roast	$7.49 /lb
	Rump Roast	$3.99 /lb
	Round Tip Steak	$1.99 /lb
	Minute Steak	$4.90 /lb
	Round Steak	$4.39 /lb
Shank and Brisket area	Whole Brisket	$4.19 /lb
Plate area (below rib area)	Skirt Steak	$3.99/lb
	Fajita Meat	$4.69 /lb
Flank Area (below short loin area)	Flank Steak	$4.99 /lb
	Flank Steak Fillet	$7.49 /lb

Preparing beef and veal for freezing

Preparing meat for the freezer is not a difficult task. There are several practical things to think about to ensure your beef does well in storage in the freezer.

- Cut the meat into portion sizes that will feed your family for one meal when the package comes out of the freezer. This will help reduce the chances for waste.

- Use packaging that is designed for use in the freezer. Freezer bags are made of thicker material than sandwich bags and will resist tearing to provide protection from freezer burn. Plastic freezer containers are also designed to protect frozen foods from freezer burn and from the absorption of excess moisture that accumulates when the freezer door is opened and the temperature in the freezer raises.

- Do your best to remove all the air from freezer bags. Air that remains in the freezer bag will contribute to frozen food drying out and going stale.

- Make sure the package is sealed completely to reduce chances for freezer burn. Freezer burn causes discoloration of the surface of the meat. Although freezer burn does not make the product inedible, it does give meat an unappetizing appearance. The discoloration is an indication that the meat has absorbed excess moisture and has been affected by the temperature fluctuations of the opening and closing of the freezer door. Removing unnecessary moisture reduces the chance for ice crystals to form over long-term storage.

- Be sure to label packages to eliminate the chances of losing track of what you have in the freezer. Labels help you use food before it reaches its safe storage life.

If the electricity goes out, do not despair. Resist opening the freezer door unless it is absolutely necessary. If the freezer remains closed, the contents will stay frozen for several hours, even if there is no electricity running to keep a constant temperature. A good practice may be to keep a big block of ice on the bottom shelf of the freezer for just such emergencies. Just like the old days, large blocks of ice remain frozen in an insulated and closed container, and this may allow your food to remain frozen for up to five days if the freezer door remains closed.

HINTS FOR CANNING BEEF AND VEAL

1.   Beef and veal must always be processed in a pressure canner according to established procedures to ensure your finished product is safe to eat. The steam and pressure in a pressure canner brings the temperature to 240, which is the safe processing temperature for low-acid foods such as meat.

2.   Always use canning jars to process meat because they are manufactured to stronger standards than jars used for mayonnaise and other commercially processed food. Canning jars will not break or crack under the pressures that are exerted in a pressure canner.

3.   Stew meat is the easiest product for the beginning canner to start with. Stew meat is already cut into small pieces that are ready for processing.

4.   To make stew meat, cut across the grain of the beef cut you are working with. Begin by cutting the meat into 1-inch strips; then cut the strips into cubes. The smaller pieces are easier to get into canning jars.

5.   When cutting a piece of beef, it is best to remove as much fat and gristle as possible. The next step is to remove as much white muscle covering as possible.

6.   If you are working with a piece of meat that has a bone, cut as closely as possible to the bone without getting bone chunks or slivers into your meat.

7.   Partially precook beef to seal in moisture and flavor by simmering or frying to a rare condition.

8.   When filling canning jars with the meat, be careful to ensure fat and grease does not build up on the lip of the jar. Fat and grease on the lip may impede the lid making a good seal.

Recipes

Instructions for canning beef stew meat

1. Either use pre-cut, packaged stew meat or cut your own. If you are going to use quart jars, estimate using 3 to 4 pounds of fresh meat per jar and half of that for pint jars.

2. If you are cutting your own stew meat, remove all excess fat and gristle from the meat along with the white muscle covering and cut into 1-inch cubes, cutting across the grain of meat.

3. The meat can be precooked, although it is not absolutely necessary to precook the meat for this recipe.

4. If canning meat that has not been precooked, it is not necessary to add liquid to the meat when it is packed in the canning jars. The meat will produce its own juice during the time in the pressure canner.

5. A beef broth should be added to meat that has been precooked when the meat is packed into the canning jars.

6. Pack the meat loosely in the canning jars, leaving 1 inch of headspace below the lid. It will be easier to pack the meat if you use wide-mouth jars. Remember: Do not pack the meat tightly in the jar. If the meat is packed too tightly, it may not cook thoroughly. Add salt at this time, unless you plan to salt the meat at the time that it is served. Consider using ½-teaspoon for pint jars and 1 teaspoon for quart jars.

7. Before placing lids on the jars, be sure the lips of the jars are clean and dry to facilitate the sealing process. Place lids on jars and screw on securing rings (bands). There is no need to tighten excessively as the ring is only being used to secure the lid until the vacuum in the jar seals the lid.

8. Place jars in the pressure canner, ensuring that jars do not touch each other. Fill canner with water to the level prescribed by the instructions for your canner. Process the meat for the time and pressure prescribed for your elevation. Your pressure canner should have come with a time and pressure chart.

A time and pressure adjustment chart for using a pressure canner can be found in Chapter 2.

9. For this particular recipe, the processing time using a pressure canner with a dial gauge at 2,000 feet elevation for pint jars is 75 minutes with 11 pounds of pressure. At 6,000 feet, the pressure needs to be 14 pounds. If your pressure canner has a weighted gauge, the pressure at 1,000 feet must be 10 pounds, and over 1,000 feet, the pressure must be increased to 15 pounds.

10. If you are using quart jars, the processing time must be increased to 90 minutes at the pressure adjustments already indicated.

Recipe for canning meatloaf

*This recipe was provided courtesy of David G. Blackburn of **www.canningusa.com**.*

GENERAL TIPS

1. Meatloaf recipes usually include the use of breadcrumbs or crackers as a binding agent to absorb the grease that develops when the meat is cooked. Binding agents cannot be used during the canning process because they interfere with the cooking of the meat in a pressure canner.

2. When the time comes to use the canned meatloaf, drain off the liquid, slice the meatloaf, and reheat it underneath the broiler. For sandwiches, pan fry it in a cast iron skillet and add a little grated cheese after turning.

3.   The ground pork and fresh sage in this recipe may be substituted with a pound of sage-flavored sausage. The roasted red bell pepper sauce may be substituted with a chopped and sautéed red bell pepper.

4.   This recipe may be used to make a standard, oven-baked meatloaf by adding one cup of crushed Original Wheat Thins® and baking at 350 degrees for approximately one hour.

5.   The approximate yield for this recipe is five pints. Wide-mouth jars make canning much easier. If you use a single 1-quart jar, there will be more meatloaf than you can use, so five 1-pint jars would be a more efficient use of this recipe unless you increase the ingredients to use quart jars.

INGREDIENTS

Ground beef, 15 percent fat.............2 pounds

Pork, 12 to 15 percent fat.................1 pound

Medium chopped onions 2

Large chopped tomato......................1

Roasted red bell pepper sauce ....¼ pint

Minced garlic (optional)...................1 clove

Worcestershire sauce........................2 tablespoons

Dijon mustard.................................2 tablespoons

Chopped fresh sage ....2 tablespoons

Salt..1 teaspoon

Pepper...½ teaspoon

COOKING INSTRUCTIONS

1.   Bring ingredients to room temperature.

2. *In a large bowl, mix all ingredients following the recipe for making and canning pâté provided in Chapter 5.*

3. When canning, use the raw-pack method, leaving 1 inch of headspace in the jar.

4. Process with a pressure canner for 75 minutes at 11 pounds of pressure, or 10 pounds for a weighted gauge.

5. For elevations above 1,000 feet, use an altitude and pressure adjustment chart. *A chart providing elevation adjustments for pressure and time is provided in Chapter 2 in the case study by David G. Blackburn.*

6. After processing, remove from boiling water and place the jars on a towel, separated by 1 inch, to cool naturally as quickly as possible.

7. Label and store the jars.

Beef burgundy

*This recipe was provided courtesy of David G. Blackburn of **www.canningusa.com**.*

INGREDIENTS

	DINNER	CANNING
Pot roast	Two pounds	Six pounds
Medium onions	2	6
Shallots	6	18
Fat back or bacon	Two slices	Six slices
Diced carrots	1 ½ cups	4 ½ cups
Salt	One teaspoon	Three teaspoons
Pepper	½ teaspoon	1 ½ teaspoon
Beef bullion (optional)	One cube	Three cubes
Garlic	One clove	Three cloves
Mushrooms	One pound	Three pounds

Burgundy wine...............................½ bottle	1 ½ bottle
Cognac...⅓ cup	One cup
Olive oil ....Two tablespoons	½ cup

PREPARATION INSTRUCTIONS

1. Trim the beef, brown in a heavy skillet, cover at medium heat or in the oven at 450 degrees Fahrenheit for 10 minutes, and then turn it and brown 10 minutes longer.

2. Brown the bacon with the olive oil and garlic for about seven minutes over medium heat.

3. Add the diced onions, shallots, salt, and pepper, then sauté, stirring occasionally, until the onions and shallots are translucent.

4. Add the mushrooms and bullion, then sauté about five minutes.

5. Add the beef, wine, and cognac, and simmer for about two hours.

6. Add the carrots and additional salt and pepper to taste, and then simmer about 1 ½ hours longer.

7. For canning, use the hot-pack method, leaving 1 inch of headspace at the top of the canning jars.

8. Process with a pressure canner for 75 minutes and 11 pounds of pressure, or 10 pounds of pressure for a weighted gauge.

9. *For elevations above 1,000 feet, use the adjustment chart in Chapter 2.*

BENEFITS OF CURING BEEF AND VEAL

There are many benefits for your family when you decide to cure meat in your home. Remember the curing process is designed to safely preserve meat for use at a future date. If you have meat in your home that has been preserved through curing, you will have food for your family regardless if the electricity goes out or some natural disaster cuts off access to the grocery store. The other primary benefit is that you can prepare some very flavorful and enjoyable meat products to share with your friends and extended family. Curing is a particularly useful activity if you harvest game or raise beef for your personal use.

Recipes

Recipe for dry curing beef

The following recipe is the author's creation.

Note: Beef is usually exposed to curing in preparation for smoking or drying to make jerky.

INGREDIENTS

Curing salt	10 pounds
Sugar	3 ¾ pounds
Saltpeter	2 ½ ounces
Sodium nitrate	½ to 1 ounce (excess nitrate is toxic)

Any optional seasoning you want to add in preparation for later uses of the beef.

PREPARATION INSTRUCTIONS

1. Mix the ingredients, and then rub the curing compound on the pieces of meat. Remove excess fat and gristle from the pieces of meat. Be generous with the curing mix when rubbing it on the meat.

2. Place a layer of the curing compound on the bottom of your curing box.

3. Place the meat on the bottom layer of curing mix, then pack the curing mix all around the meat. If more than one piece of meat is

being cured, make sure a complete layer of mix is laid between the pieces of meat.

4. Many people have different opinions on how soon the meat needs to be unpacked and turned over, then repacked. The meat should be taken out no later than two days after the original packing. Then the bare spots need to be rubbed, the liquid brine drained, and the meat repacked. The meat should be fully cured after one week. The meat should remain refrigerated during this curing process.

Experience gained over several curing events will enable you to refine the process to your preferences. Since the meat has not yet been cooked or hot smoked to kill microbes, the meat should remain refrigerated for safety.

ADDING FLAVOR TO BEEF AND VEAL THROUGH SMOKING

Smoking meat serves a two-fold purpose. The smoke dehydrates the meat, which removes moisture and retards bacterial growth, and the chemicals in the smoke coat the meat, inhibiting bacterial growth. Smoking is an extension of the preservation process that began when you cured your meat. After meat has been cured and smoked, it is well preserved for long-term storage and use at a later date. The other important purpose for smoking meat is to impart desired flavors to the finished product. The home smoker can create custom meat products with wonderful flavorings that will be very satisfying to your family.

The actual chemical processes that take place while meat is being smoked are very complicated. Wood smoke from hardwoods contains molecules that provide the coloring and flavoring people enjoy so much. For example, the phenolic compounds that are part of wood smoke are antioxidants that slow the process of meat turning rancid. A phenolic compound called guaiacol is responsible for the smoky flavor that people enjoy.

Treated or painted wood should not be used for meat smoking because chemicals from burning the treatment chemicals or paint will be imparted to the meat. Wood such as pine should not be used because of the high resin concentration in the wood. Burning resinous wood would impart undesirable taste and qualities to food products.

Recipes

Smoked beef summer sausage

The following recipe is the author's creation.

INGREDIENTS

Lean meat ....15 pounds
Beef fat...2 ¾ pounds
Water ....4 ¼ cups
Dried milk ....3 ¾ cups
Sugar..⅓ cup
Salt...¾ cup
Onion powder...................................1 teaspoon
Garlic powder....................................½ teaspoon
Mustard seed ....⅓ cup
Pepper..4 tablespoons
Liquid smoke ....2 tablespoons
Cure...4 level teaspoons
Sodium erythorbate...........................2 teaspoons

A manual or electric meat grinder with grinding plates will be needed, as will a smokehouse capable of heating products to 185 degrees Fahrenheit.

SPECIAL CONSIDERATIONS

1. Beef or wild game such as deer or elk may be used.

2. Use more or less beef fat, depending on how lean or fatty the meat being used is.

3. Adjust the level of salt used depending on taste. If you have allergies to specific spices, simply leave out the spice you cannot tolerate and replace it with a suitable substitute.

4. Do not overuse mustard seed, as it will change the flavor of your product significantly. Ground mustard mixes do not replace mustard seed very well in this type of recipe.

5. Use more or less pepper to meet individual taste expectations.

6. Use slightly less liquid smoke to reduce strong smoke flavor in the finished product.

7. Cure is manufactured by different companies under different names. Some cure products are designed to impart specific flavoring to the finished product. Select a curing product that will produce the finished taste you are looking for.

8. If you do not have access to a meat grinder and decide to use commercially ground meat, use ground beef that has 7 percent fat or less. If you are using lean wild game, remember that if the meat is very lean, it would be best to add additional beef fat. If the product is too dry, the meat will not bind as desired to make sausage.

PREPARATION INSTRUCTIONS

1. Grind the meat and fat. The size of plate used will determine the coarseness of the finished product. Normal sausage grinding requires the use of a ½-inch plate. You can use a smaller or larger grinding plate depending on your desire for a finer or coarser finished product.

2. The liquid smoke, cure, and sodium erythorbate should be mixed together in the 4 ¼ cups of water.

3. Combine all of the ingredients together and stuff into natural sausage casings. Natural casings are preferred over synthetic products.

4. Cook the product in a smokehouse, maintaining a temperature of 185 degrees Fahrenheit. It is very important to keep a constant temperature throughout the cooking process to maintain the quality of the finished product.

5. Heat the sausage until the meat has an internal temperature of at least 152 degrees Fahrenheit. This is very important to insure that all dangerous bacterium is destroyed.

6. After the meat is cooked, the temperature must be reduced to 90 degrees to stop the cooking process and allow the final curing process to take place. The temperature is usually reduced by showering the product with water until it is reduced to a temperature of 90 degrees Fahrenheit. Then you should allow the sausage to hang at room temperature for about an hour, but no more than two hours before refrigerating the product.

Italian hot sausage

This recipe was provided courtesy of North Dakota State University Extension and Julie Garden-Robinson.

INGREDIENTS

Lean beef trim
   (Beef trim is available at your butcher shop).............5 pounds
Pork trim 60/40 (60 percent meat, 40 percent fat) ......5 pounds
Garlic cloves, crushed...20

Red pepper...4 teaspoons

Fennel seeds, crushed ....4 teaspoons

Thyme...2 teaspoons

Bay leaves..8

Salt..3 tablespoons

Black pepper ....1 tablespoon

Nutmeg...½ teaspoon

PREPARATION INSTRUCTIONS

1. Grind meat through a coarse grinding plate.

2. Add spices and mix all the ingredients together thoroughly.

3. Grind again through a medium grinding plate.

4. Stuff mixture into a hog casing.

5. Smoke at 140 degrees for proper color development and then raise temperature to 170 degrees until the internal temperature of the product reaches 155 degrees.

6. This is a very hot and spicy product. It is excellent on pizza and will substitute for pepperoni.

Is sausage preparation considered preservation?

There is some controversy over the words preparation and preservation as the words relate to sausage. Beef is an important element in the production of various styles of sausage. Either ground beef or beef tallow is mixed with various other meats, such as venison, pork, or even goat, to produce a wide variety of wonderful sausages. Tallow is beef fat that has been rendered — that is, heated at temperatures less than boiling. Tallow is solid at room temperature and can be stored in an airtight container for long periods.

There is no doubt that sausage is a prepared food. Sausage is a mixture of meats, spices, and curing agents stuffed into casings produced from proteins derived from beef or pig hides. Modern science discovered that proteins called collagen, which can be derived from animal hides, could be broken down and reconstituted into a mass which can be made into a tube or casing for sausage. Collagen-based casings go through an extensive process to ensure the product is sanitary and suitable for use with food for human consumption.

The root for the word sausage comes from the Latin word "salsus," which is defined as salted or preserved. To determine if sausage is a preserved meat product, you must understand what the preservation process is. From all that has already been written in this book, you understand that preservation processes inhibit the growth of microorganisms that would normally lead to foodborne illnesses in humans. Some techniques used in sausage making are the same as those used in the meat preservation process. Freezing, smoking, and curing are meat preservation processes, so the making of sausage falls under the category of meat preservation.

TIPS FOR MEAT GRINDING, SAUSAGE MAKING, AND SMOKING

1. When you purchase a meat grinder for making sausage, you will also need a sausage stuffer. Sausage stuffers quickly put the mixed meat through a casing, with minimal air pockets, using less time and energy. This lessens the time the meat is exposed to air, which could promote bacteria growth.

2. Meat grinder plates come in a variety of sizes. Different recipes will require the grinding of meat to prepare your meat product for

mixing and stuffing into sausage casings. Meat grinder plates come in the following sizes: ³⁄₃₂, ⅛, ⁵⁄₃₂, ³⁄₁₆, ¼, ⅜, ½, and ¾. The ³⁄₃₂-inch produces a real fine ground meat product, and the ¾-inch size will produce a coarse ground meat product.

3. Moving your ground meat quickly from the grinder into the sausage casing is very important. A casing stuffing horn is an important tool that will aid in this process. Stuffing horns are either straight or tapered and come in a variety of sizes. The following charts will assist you in selecting the correct size of horn for the size of casings you plan to use.

Straight Horn Applications

Size of Casing Being Used	Horn Size Required
16 mm	⅜ inch
19 mm	⁷⁄₁₆ inch
21 mm	⁷⁄₁₆ inch
23 mm	½ inch
28 mm	⁹⁄₁₆ inch
30 mm	⁹⁄₁₆ inch
32 mm	⁹⁄₁₆ inch
35 mm	¾ inch

Tapered Horn Applications

Size of Casing Being used	Type of Casing Being Used	Horn Size Required
21 and 23 mm	collagen	½ inch
22 to 24 mm	sheep	½ inch
28, 30, 32 mm	collagen	½ inch
32 to 35 mm	hog	¾ inch

4. Successful sausage making requires high-quality sausage casings. The casings are usually cleaned animal intestines or processed collagen. They can also sometimes be made of a synthetic material that can withstand high temperatures with no reactions.

5. People who consider themselves traditional sausage makers primarily use natural casings. Natural casings are made from sheep, hog, and beef intestinal materials that have been fully flushed and sanitized and are completely safe for human consumption. They give sausage its well-known crackle in every bite and take on different colors depending on the smoking techniques used. The process takes patience, but serious sausage makers say it is worth it.

Commonly used sausage casings

1. Sheep casings are used for sausage products that are considered tender, such as fresh breakfast sausage.

2. Hog casings are popular and can be used for any ground meat product. This is the easiest natural casing product to find on the commercial market.

3. Beef casings are used for products that need a strong, thick casing.

4. Collagen casings are made from materials derived from the bones and cartilage of animals. This is the most widely used sausage casing in the United States.

5. Synthetic casing does not need to be refrigerated. Synthetic casing is used by mass producers and comes in different colors to aid in the identification of different sausage products.

ADDITIONAL SAFETY ISSUES WHEN PRESERVING BEEF AND VEAL

1. Beef products should be selected just before going to the grocery checkout so they do not end up sitting in the grocery cart for 30 minutes or more without refrigeration.

2. Unfrozen beef sitting in the refrigerator should be used within three to five days. Uncooked beef stored in the refrigerator for periods longer than five days will spoil.

3. Never brown or precook beef and put it back in the refrigerator for later cooking. Bacteria that were not destroyed during the browning will grow and possibly lead to foodborne disease.

4. Do not exceed the level of nitrite that is listed in any recipe you decide to try, because excessive consumption of nitrite can be lethal. A good recommendation for home meat preservers is to use salt-sodium nitrite mixtures that are readily available for purchase from companies providing products for home meat preservers. If you feel you must include nitrite in a recipe on your own, there are some drug stores that may weigh out the appropriate amount for a particular recipe. Just remember to be careful when you decide to add nitrite or nitrate to a recipe. It can serve a useful purpose in your meat preservation efforts as long as these elements are used exactly as the recipe requires.

CHAPTER 4:
Preserving Poultry for the Family

Chickens, turkeys, and many other game birds make up a substantial portion of the world's meat diet. These animals are easy to keep and are a great way for the families with limited space to teach children about responsibility and the value of raising your own food. Because of this, a major focus of this chapter will be providing information that will help people know how to safely handle poultry products. Many people have become very sick from diseases that come from the improper handling and preparation of poultry products.

VARIETIES OF POULTRY

When most people think of the word poultry, they are thinking of chickens, ducks, and turkeys. The word poultry covers a much broader range of birds than the domestic birds people are most familiar with. The following list will provide a sample of the wider range of bird types that are considered poultry.

Common Poultry

Type	Products
Chicken	meat, feathers, eggs
Duck	meat, feathers, eggs
Emu	meat, leather, oil
Goose	meat, feathers, eggs
Ostrich	meat, feathers, leather
Turkey	meat, feathers
Guinea fowl	meat
Pheasant	meat

Bear in mind that some recipes will allow the use of different poultry types, and some recipes are only applicable to a particular type of bird. Do not be afraid to experiment. The important point to remember is that poultry provides lean meat and must be cooked accordingly.

Domestic poultry

The following list provides information on poultry that can be commonly found throughout the country. Some of the game bird varieties are not available in all areas of the country.

Chickens

1. **New Hampshire:** These birds have deep and broad bodies with an adult weight of about 6 ½ pounds. They work well as a broiler or as a roasting bird.

2. **Plymouth barred rock:** These birds are used to produce both meat and eggs. They have a long back with a moderately full breast. The birds have yellow skin and legs.

3. **Silver laced wyandotte:** These birds lay around 220 eggs per year. Adult males get weigh in at 8 ½ pounds. They are considered good producers of eggs and meat.

4. **Jersey giant:** Mature roosters can weigh in as 13 pounds, with hens weighing 11 pounds. They grow a large frame early in their life and flesh out as they mature. They lay extra-large brown eggs.

5. **Dominique:** These birds are known for both their egg and meat production. They lay a brown egg and weigh in at 6 to 8 pounds.

6. **Rhode Island red:** Considered a good utility bird that is resistant to illness and very hardy, these birds are good backyard foraging birds. They can produce up to 300 brown eggs per year. Roosters weigh in at 8 ½ pounds with hens at 6 ½ pounds.

7. **Cornish game hen:** These birds are actually chickens that are slaughtered at a young age. They are not game birds. Both males and females are sold under the title Cornish game hen. They are always sold as a whole bird.

Turkeys and Domestic Geese

1. **Narragansett:** Good egg producers with excellent quality meat. Usually do not wander far from home, making them a good choice for home production. Young toms weigh in at 22 to 28 pounds, with hens at 12 to 16 pounds. The word "tom" designates a male bird. The female is a "hen."

2. **Broad-breasted white:** The most widely used turkey in commercial production. They produce more breast meat than other breeds. At 24 weeks, young toms weigh in at up to 40 pounds, with females weighing up to 20 pounds at 20 weeks of age.

3. **Domestic geese:** Embden is a variety raised in Europe and North America, with males weighing in at up to 22 pounds and females weighing up to 20 pounds. A variety of goose that is declining in popularity is the Pilgrim, with males weighing in at up to 13 pounds and females weighing 11 to 12 pounds.

Common Game Birds

1. **Ring neck pheasant:** One of the most hunted upland game birds in the United States. They are the State Bird of South Dakota. They are ground feeders, eating insects and seeds.

2. **Ruffed grouse:** Also called partridge in some areas of the country. Found in the Appalachian Mountains and most of Canada. A very easy animal to clean after it has been harvested.

3. **Spruce grouse:** Found in Northern Canada and Alaska. They depend on their coloring to hide and many times do not take flight when approached by a hunter. They eat spruce buds in the fall and winter and take on a spruce-like taste.

4. **Blue grouse:** The largest member of the grouse family, they are found in the Rocky Mountains and the Pacific Coast Range.

5. **Bobwhite quail:** Also known as Northern Bobwhite or Virginia quail. Found from Florida to the upper Midwest. They are difficult to hunt because of their excellent camouflage.

6. **California Valley quail:** This bird is found mainly in the Southwest. This is the State Bird of California.

7. **Scaled quail:** This bird is found in desert regions of the Southwest. This bird has healthier populations than most other quail species.

8. **Eastern turkey:** Also known simply as "wild turkey." They are found throughout the eastern half of the United States and Canada. They are cautious birds that are hard to hunt, but their size will feed the whole family.

9. **Gould's turkey:** Found in Arizona and New Mexico and other mountainous areas. They have very long legs and unusually large feet.

Waterfowl

There are so many varieties of ducks that many species will be listed here for your convenience. Duck species in North America include: wood duck, green-winged teal, American black duck, mallard, Northern pintail, gadwall, canvasback, common goldeneye, hooded and common merganser, and the ruddy duck. In many cases, states that have duck hunting seasons have specific bag limits on the different species of ducks, so you must be careful when hunting to properly identify which bird you are looking at before you pull the trigger.

There are also several varieties of geese in North America that are hunted; the most popular is the Canada goose, which weighs in at 9–10 pounds, the Graylag goose weighs in at 7–8 pounds, the snow goose weighs in at 7–8 pounds, the blue goose, which is a dark color phase of the snow goose, and the Ross's goose, which looks very much like the snow goose. Again, being able to correctly identify which bird you are looking at when hunting is important.

SPECIAL FOOD HANDLING PRECAUTIONS FOR POULTRY

With all of the different types of domestic and wild birds that have been listed, it is apparent that poultry has been and will remain a major food source for the country. Although most people consume chicken, turkey, or some other type of fowl several times each week, there are a significant number of food safety concerns that need to be addressed by the home meat preserver. The four bacteria that must be controlled in poultry preparation are as follows:

- **Salmonella** comes from the intestinal tracts of animals. It is important to keep internal organs removed from the animals away from contact with the meat.

- **Staphylococcus** is found in foods improperly refrigerated, like chicken salad. It can be carried on human hands, in nasal passages, or in human throats.

- **Campylobacter Jejuni** is the most common producer of diarrheal sickness in humans. It is easily transmitted by the cross contamination of foods.

- **Listeria Monocytogenes** was discovered in 1981. It can be spread by not washing hands after handling poultry. It can be controlled by proper refrigeration of poultry.

The keys to preventing the spread and growth of these organisms are proper refrigeration, sanitary food handling techniques, and proper cooking temperatures. The meat must reach an internal temperature of at least 165 degrees that is measured with an internal meat thermometer. The handling procedures for turkey and domestic geese are the same as for chicken.

There are several precautions to take when handling game birds and waterfowl:

- Do not handle game that is obviously sick.
- Use latex gloves when field dressing game.
- Any old wounds that you find in game must be cut away during cleaning. If in doubt as to the safety of the meat, do not keep the animal for human consumption.
- Keep intestinal tract organs away from the meat during field dressing.
- Wash hands immediately after cleaning the animal with a strong alcohol-based sanitizer.
- Make sure field dressing and cleaning tools and equipment are thoroughly washed and sanitized before you put them away.
- Do not eat raw or undercooked game.

Chicken is America's favorite meat.

FREEZING POULTRY AND EGGS

The following procedures for freezing poultry are intended to prepare the meat so that when it is removed from the freezer at a later date, it can be easily thawed out and cooked for your family's enjoyment.

Whole birds: Lock wings and fold neck skin over wing tips. Tie legs and pad the ends with paper to prevent them from puncturing the wrapping. Wrap in moisture/vapor-proof paper or use a plastic bag, pressing out as much air as possible.

Pieces of poultry: Flatten pieces and place double thickness of wrapping material between pieces for easy separation. Pad sharp ends of bones. Wrap in freezer paper or place in plastic bags or containers.

Giblets (except livers): Giblets are the internal parts of the bird that are edible such as the heart, liver, and gizzard (a muscular pouch behind the stomach). Package these separately and use within three months. Package livers together and use within one month.

Game birds: Although wild game is prepared for freezing as domestic poultry, there are a few extra precautions that are necessary for optimum results. Newly shot birds should not be placed in waterproof pockets of hunting jackets, since the waterproof material will not allow the birds to cool out as they should. If the animal does not cool out completely, it is more prone to bacterial growth. If the trip home is long, the birds should at least have their craws and intestines removed. The craw is the area below the neck where the bird stores food. This area is loaded with bacteria that should be removed from the bird to keep bacteria from spreading to the rest of the animal. A recommended flavor-saver is to soak them overnight in a 2-gallon vessel of water mixed with ½-cup vinegar. After birds have been drawn, plucked, and washed carefully inside and out, chill thoroughly, and then treat as domestic poultry.

Whole eggs: Freeze whole eggs, some with salt added for scrambling, omelets, or meat mixtures; some with sugar for cakes or custards. Eggs must be removed from the shell and mixed well before freezing. They can be kept in the freezer for up to a year.

1. Gently mix whites and yolks.
2. Add 1 teaspoon of salt or 1 tablespoon of sugar or corn syrup for each 2 cups of eggs. The addition of sugar and salt before freezing whole eggs or yolks is essential to prevent gumminess when the egg is thawed out.

Egg yolks: Separate egg yolks from whites. Break yolks; mix thoroughly with 2 teaspoons of sugar or corn syrup for each 2 cups of yolks. Do not whip in air.

Egg whites: Nothing needs to be added.

TO PACKAGE EGGS FOR FREEZING:
1. Fill containers, leaving headspace and seal.
2. Label each package indicating the amount, the addition of salt or sweetening, and date.
3. To thaw, place container in cold water. Use within 12 hours after thawing.

EQUIVALENTS:
1. Two tablespoons thawed white is equal to one egg white.
2. One and one third tablespoons thawed yolk is equal to one egg yolk.
3. Three tablespoons thawed whole egg is equal to one whole egg.

PUTTING THE CHICKEN IN A JAR

When canning chicken, it is always best to use the freshest birds possible. If the chicken has been freshly slaughtered and dressed, it is best to set it in the refrigerator to chill for six to 12 hours before canning. Usually, large chickens provide better flavor after they are removed from the jar than fryers do. A chicken classified as a fryer has been slaughtered at nine to 12 weeks and weighs about three to four pounds.

Cut the chicken into sizes that will fit into the size of jar you are planning to use, either pints or quarts. Chicken may be canned with or without the bones. Chicken can be hot packed or raw packed. If you choose to hot pack the chicken, precook by boiling, steaming, or baking until the bird is two-thirds of the way done. Add up to 1 teaspoon of salt per quart jar if desired. Fill the jars with chicken pieces and hot broth from the cooking process, leaving 1 ¼-inch of headspace. Install lids and bands and place in pressure canner.

If you choose to raw pack the chicken, add 1 teaspoon of salt per quart jar if desired, and loosely pack the chicken in the jar. Do not add liquid when raw packing the meat. Always leave 1 ¼-inch of headspace in the jar. Install lids and bands and place in pressure canner.

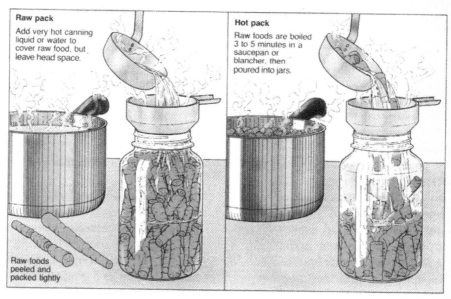

You can either hot pack or raw pack chicken.
Image courtesy of the USDA.

Follow the chart provided with your pressure canner that lists the time and pressure food should be processed at for your elevation, or you can refer to the following chart.

Chicken Processing Chart for a Dial Gauge Pressure Canner

	Jar Size	Processing Time	0 to 2,000 ft	2,001 to 4,000 ft	4,001 to 6,000 ft	6,001 to 8,000 ft
Bones in Meat Hot and Raw	Pint	75 min.	11 lb	12 lb	13 lb	14 lb
	Quart:	90 min.	11 lb	12 lb	13 lb	14 lb
No Bones Hot and Raw	Pint	65 min.	11 lb	12 lb	13 lb	14 lb
	Quart	75 min.	11 lb	12 lb	13 lb	14 lb

Note: Hot designates meat that has been precooked, and raw designates meat that has not been heated or cooked. The difference in preparing hot and raw comes with the amount of moisture that is added to the canning jar. This difference in added moisture will be indicated in the specific recipe you are using.

Chicken Processing Chart for a Weighted Gauge Pressure Canner

	Jar Size	Processing Time	0 to 1000 ft	above 1000 ft
Bones in Meat Hot and Raw	Pint	75 min	10 lb	15 lb
	Quart	90 min	10 lb	15 lb
No Bones Hot and Raw	Pint	65 min	10 lb	15 lb
	Quart	65 min	10 lb	15 lb

Recipes

Poultry canning recipes involve adding additional spices to the product to enhance the flavor when the meat is served. Other good recipes involve putting the canned chicken with the entire meal presentation.

Canning chicken and onions

*This recipe was provided courtesy of David G. Blackburn of **www.canningusa. com**.*

INGREDIENTS (MAKES EIGHT QUARTS)

Chicken cut into pieces ....16 pounds

Onions, peeled and sliced.................16 pounds, or less to your preference

Salt..2 tablespoons

Pepper...2 tablespoons

Olive oil ....¼ cup

COOKING INSTRUCTIONS

1. Brown deboned and skinless chicken in a large skillet using olive oil on medium heat for approximately five minutes per side. Add salt and pepper. You may need to use an additional skillet. After browning, combine in one pot.

2. Add onions, cover, and cook at simmer for 1 ½ hours or until onions are caramelized.

3. For canning, use hot-pack method with 1-inch headspace in the jars.

4. Process with pressure canner for 75 minutes at 11 pounds of pressure, or 10 pounds for a weighted gauge.

5. *For elevations above 1000 feet, use the time and pressure adjustment chart provided in Chapter 2.*

PREPARING POULTRY FOR CURING

Poultry will be prepared for curing in much the same way as other types of meat. Remember the discussion earlier in the chapter about precautions to take to avoid cross contamination with other food products when handling fresh poultry. Until poultry is cooked to at least 165 degrees Fahrenheit, it may contain dangerous bacteria. Curing does not cook meat, so remember the poultry will still need to be heated to the proper temperature before it is consumed. Hot smoking techniques can raise the internal temperature of the meat to the safe level.

Recipes

Dry cure compound

In Chapter 3, a formulation for a dry cure compound was provided. This compound will work for any type of meat. For smaller quantities of meat, it may be advisable to cut the amount down. For example, you could halve each of the ingredients and still have a dry cure compound that will prepare your meat for smoking or drying. Just remember to add any seasoning ingredient you need for the taste you are looking to impart into your meat product.

PREPARATION INSTRUCTIONS

1. After the ingredients have been mixed well, the curing compound will be rubbed on the pieces of meat. Be generous with the curing mix.

2. Place a layer of the curing compound on the bottom of your curing box.

3. Place the meat on the bottom layer of curing mix, then pack the curing mix all around the meat. If more than one piece of meat is being cured, make sure a complete layer of mix is laid between the pieces of meat.

4. Many people have different opinions on how soon the meat needs to be unpacked and turned over, then repacked. The meat should be taken out no later than two days after the original packing. Then the bare spots need to be rubbed, the liquid brine drained, and the meat repacked. The meat should be fully cured after one week. The meat should remain refrigerated during this curing process. Experience gained over several curing events will enable you to refine the process to your preferences. Since the meat has not yet been cooked or hot smoked to kill microbes, the meat should remain refrigerated for safety.

SMOKING TURKEY AND OTHER POULTRY

Smoked turkey has been gaining popularity over the last few years. Smoked turkey has become a favorite with many families at Thanksgiving. For families that are looking for some variety in their holiday fare, a smoked turkey provides a way to preserve an element of the traditional meal, with the taste of something new and exciting. The same procedures that apply to the preparation of other meats are also applicable to smoking turkeys and other poultry. This may be a great way for you and your family to try something new for dinner. At the end of this chapter, you will find a case study on smoking turkey.

Recipes

Smoked turkey and pork sausage

This recipe was provided courtesy of North Dakota State University and Julie Garden-Robinson.

INGREDIENTS

Turkey trim (90 percent lean)	50 pounds
Pork trim (50 percent lean)	40 pounds
Water	3 quarts
Salt	3 cups
Dextrose	1 cup to 1 cup and 2 tablespoons
Cure	6 tablespoons
White pepper	1 cup
Sage	½ cup

Cayenne ....¼ cup

Thyme ....1 tablespoon

Nutmeg ....1 tablespoon

Ginger ....1 tablespoon

Mace ....1 tablespoon

Monosodium glutamate (optional) ....10 tablespoons

PREPARATION INSTRUCTIONS

1. Coarse-grind meat trimmings.

2. Add water, salt, dextrose, cure, and spices.

3. Regrind through ¼-inch diameter plate.

4. Stuff into pork casings.

5. Smoke product to desired color and heat to and internal temperature of 141 degrees Fahrenheit.

6. Product must be cooked before serving. It will need to be kept under refrigeration.

7. The recipe calls for larger amounts of meat than many people will have, so you could easily halve this recipe.

SAFETY ISSUES WHEN PRESERVING POULTRY

There are a number of precautions and special considerations to take when preparing poultry for smoking. The following list itemizes some of the things you need to consider before lighting up the smoker.

1. Never defrost poultry at room temperature. Use the refrigerator to defrost your poultry at a temperature that will not allow bacteria to

grow. This will take a little time and will take some advance planning to get everything ready at the same time.

2.   If you decide to use the microwave to defrost poultry, smoke the meat immediately because some of the meat may have begun to cook during the defrosting cycle.

3.   There are two other ways that poultry can be properly defrosted using clean, cold water. You can completely submerge your bird in an airtight package. If you use this method, the water should be changed at 30-minute intervals. Another method: Using an airtight package, hold your bird under constantly running water. Cook the bird immediately after it is completely thawed.

4.   Poultry must be marinated in the refrigerator to inhibit the growth of bacteria. If some of the marinating sauce is to be used to baste the bird, keep some separate for later use. Do not put raw poultry in the sauce being reserved for basting. Never reuse marinating sauce unless it is boiled to at least 165 degrees Fahrenheit to kill bacteria.

5.   If you are using a homemade smoker, make sure it is cleaned of all chemical residues and completely sanitary.

6.   A safe temperature for your hot smoker when smoking poultry is between 225 to 300 degrees Fahrenheit.

7.   When the poultry is done smoking, put it into the refrigerator within two hours. Use the smoked poultry within four days or freeze for later use.

CASE STUDY: HOW TO SMOKE TURKEY

Brad Bolton
What's Cooking America?
http://whatscookingamerica.net

This case study is adopted from the "What's Cooking America?" Web site, courtesy of Brad Bolton.

The first step in doing a turkey on a smoker is to pick out a bird that is not the biggest one you can find. The main reason for a smaller bird, 10 to 14 pounds maximum, is the time limitation usually involved. It takes between six and eight hours to smoke a 12-pound turkey, and the bigger they get, the longer they take.

Next, set up the smoker. When using charcoal, it is best to let the flames burn out, fill the water pan with water — seasoning is fine, too — and then place the lid on the smoker and wait for the temperature to reach the "safe" zone on your smoker. Once that is accomplished, toss the turkey on there gently and cover the smoker. Start timing the turkey when the temperature returns to the safe zone.

Safety reminder: Chickens and turkeys are prone to salmonella bacteria, which can ruin your whole Thanksgiving. Internal cooking temperatures of 165 degrees Fahrenheit minimum are essential for destroying these bacteria. This temperature is not the outside of the turkey, but the inside, so keep that in mind when you decide on a larger bird.

SMOKING TURKEY NOTES AND TIPS:

I use a water smoker, which keeps the meat moist and prevents burning like a traditional smoker, in case you forget about the turkey for a half hour or so.

I have used both inexpensive and expensive charcoal and have found the main difference to be the number of times you need to add charcoal. The better the charcoal, the longer you can wait to add more. You can expect to use 10 pounds or more of charcoal for a 10 to 14 pound turkey, so have some extra just in case.

You will most likely not have to check the charcoal or temperature for three hours if you use good charcoal, so this gives you time to watch a football game and be with the family and guests.

When you check the temperature on your smoker, just look at the gauge. Most of them have a "safe" zone or an actual readout. Be sure to keep the temperature in that safe zone.

When you add charcoal to the smoker, stir the ashes around and bring up the hot coals away from the ashes. This will help start the added charcoal faster and keep the temperature correct. Add plenty of charcoal at the beginning, and when you add more, add as much as you can.

Check the water after you add charcoal each time so you do not let it run out. If you need to add water, pour it carefully so as not to splash the hot charcoals. Try holding the water away from you to avoid steam, just in case.

It is also possible to use hickory, mesquite, or other chips in your charcoal to flavor the bird. Soak them for at least one hour in water, and then toss them on the charcoal to send smoke to your turkey.

After about five hours, it is a good idea to actually take off the lid and check the condition of the turkey. Each time you remove the lid, it adds between 10 and 15 minutes to the cook time, so do not take the lid off until you absolutely have to.

When checking the bird, you want the meat to have a pink, moist, cooked look to it. It is difficult to tell when the turkey is actually done without sampling it, of course, so use a big knife and cut into the thickest part of the breast to check.

A deep cut into the breast will tell you if it is done there, and when the breast is done, the rest of the turkey is done also. Juices are always present and should be clear when cut, but the true test is the taste test. If it seems chewy, then it is probably not done, but if it seems moist and tender, then your bird is ready for the table.

Smoking a turkey is no different from barbecuing in your back yard. You follow the rules without even thinking about them in most cases. So give it a try; you will not be dissatisfied when you try a smoked turkey. Just be sure to follow the safety rules without deviation.

If you have a larger bird or do not have six to eight hours to wait for the turkey to smoke, cut the bird up and cook it as you would a chicken. Most smokers have two racks or more, so distribute the parts evenly on each rack. I feed a small army here at Thanksgiving and Christmas, so I generally cut it into pieces and smoke it that way, which does take about half the time. It is not as pretty when it comes off the smoker, but the taste is still the same.

For those of you who have electric smokers and gas smokers, follow the instructions that came with your smoker for cooking times.

CHAPTER 5:
Preserving the Pork

People began raising pigs for food at least 9,000 years ago. Although there has been a significant technological change in the way pork is handled in the modern world, the actual methods used to raise pigs have not changed much over the years. Pigs provide farmers with the opportunity to produce a large number of animals in a relatively small amount of space. In 2006, hog finishing facilities in the United States purchased 6 million weanling pigs from Canada alone. Hog production is a major international agricultural industry. An important part of this chapter will be to discuss how people can be sure they have cooked pork completely enough to kill the trichinosis parasite. This chapter will also present some wonderful recipes and other directions for preserving pork.

Over the centuries, people have had a long-standing relationship with salt pork. In situations where no refrigeration is available, the use of salted pork still provides a relatively safe method for preserving a food source for long-term availability. Salt pork is still an important commodity for the home preserver using smoking and drying methods to preserve meat. Preserving pork is an art that people can enjoy and at the same time be involved in keeping valuable meat preservation traditions alive.

*Take a trip to the meat market to see
all different cuts of pork.*

DIFFERENCES IN DOMESTIC PORK AND WILD PORK

The rapid population growth of wild pigs has become a real problem in some areas of the United States. Wild pigs are known for destroying crops and pastureland. They have even been known to tear up country roads. Many wild boars that are killed by hunters are not fit to eat and are disposed of immediately. The meat from older, larger wild boars will be much tougher than young animals and will have a very rank taste if careful preparation methods are not used. Some people have tried soaking the meat in vinegar or a salt solution in the refrigerator in an attempt to remove some of the unpleasant smell. The best course if you want to kill a wild pig for the family is to stick with smaller, younger animals.

Some people living on small homesteads have captured wild pigs and are raising them as domestic pigs. Adult wild boars produce a very pungent odor and are best slaughtered before they reach 40 pounds. Wild pork will have a flavor that is more related to the wild foods they eat and may be leaner than domestic pork. The same food safety standards that apply to domestic pork also apply to the handling of wild pork. The main thing to remember is to cook the meat thoroughly to ensure the internal temperature of the meat reaches the safe cooking temperature for the cut of meat you are working with.

PRESERVING PORK IN THE FREEZER

General freezing instructions are much the same as for other meats. Pork products can be removed directly from the freezer and cooked without defrosting. Additional cooking time must be added to the recipe if using frozen meat. Large items such as a pork roast will take 50 percent more of the original cooking time to ensure the meat is cooked sufficiently. Additional cooking time for smaller cuts depends on the thickness and overall size of the product. Frozen cuts that are broiled should be kept as far as possible from the heat source to avoid browning too fast.

Safe freezing times for pork

1. Pork Roasts ....Store up to eight months
2. Pork Chops ....Store up to four months
3. Ground Pork...Store up to four months
4. Pork Bacon...Store up to one month
5. Ham...Store up to two months
6. Pork Lunch Meat ....Store up to two months
7. Pork Sausage..Store up to two months
8. Cooked Pork Sausage ....Store up to two months

Kay Tomaszewski provided the following insights to consider when freezing pork:

"Freezing the product slows spoilage, but you can actually spoil a product if it is kept in the home freezer too long," Kay said. "Home freezers are usually kept at zero degrees. Commercial freezers are kept around -25 degrees, which can stop spoilage. Many people think that because a meat or sausage is smoked it lasts longer, but it should be treated like any other meat."

CANNED AND PICKLED PORK

Improper handling and processing of foods such as pork in home meat preservation processes can lead to serious illness and even death from foodborne diseases. Please follow all established food safety procedures. If in doubt, do some research and be ready to ask plenty of questions. Canning jars are made in six sizes: 4-gallon, 1-gallon, ½-gallon, quarts, pints, and ½-pints. The sizes that are used most of the time for canning meats are quarts and pints. For most people canning meat at home, even the 1-gallon size would be impractical due to the size of the pressure canner that would be needed to properly can low-acid foods like meat.

Pickling involves placing meat or any other food in a brine similar to a formula you would use before smoking meat. In addition to the basic brine, pickling formulas add vinegar, sugar, and other spices. Pickling is really a fermentation process that lowers the pH level in food. The lower the pH level, the higher the acidity level will be.

Recipes

Canned pork pâté

*This recipe was provided courtesy of David G. Blackburn of **www.canningusa.com**. Approximate yield for this recipe in wide mouth jars should be 12 ½-pint jars, or 6 pints.*

INGREDIENTS

Pork with 12 to 15 percent fat..........4 pounds

Chicken liver....................................1¼ pounds

Medium onions...............................5

Shallots..3

Salt..1 tablespoon

Pepper...½ tablespoon

PREPARATION INSTRUCTIONS

1. The ingredients should be at room temperature before starting the process.

2. Grind the meat, liver, and onions. Do not include spices in this step.

3. Mix all the ingredients in a very large bowl using your hands to ensure that everything is thoroughly mixed. Include spices in this step.

4. Spoon the pâté into the jars using the raw pack method, leaving 1 inch of headspace.

5. Process in a pressure canner 75 minutes at 11 pounds, or 10 pounds for a weighted gauge.

6. *For elevations above 1,000 feet, use the time and pressure adjustment chart provided in Chapter 2.*

7. After processing, allow the pressure to reduce, remove the jars from the boiling water, and set on a towel, leaving 1 inch between the jars, and allow them to naturally cool and seal.

SPECIAL INSTRUCTIONS

1. Let the canned pâté set and age for three months before opening it. The product becomes more flavorful with a little aging.

2. If you make a sufficient quantity, you can let it age for one year to enhance flavor development.

3. If you cannot wait to taste it, go ahead and open a jar.

4. It is okay to alter the recipe slightly, adding fresh garlic or herbs, but be cautious and add herbs and spices sparingly as their flavors will intensify over time and may become overpowering. Bay leaves have this problem, and sage can become bitter.

PREPARING PORK TO LAST AWHILE THROUGH CURING

Salt pork is one of the most well-known preserved meat products in the world. A combination of factors leads to the use of salt pork products. Pigs can produce many offspring on a relatively small farm operation. Live pigs can be raised and maintained using a very diverse range of feed sources, and salt pork remains usable much longer than salt beef.

Salt pork can be made through either a dry-salt-pack process or using a salt brine solution. Salt pork is usually made from one of three primary pork cuts: pork side, pork belly, or fatback. Since salt pork comes from the same pork cuts as bacon, it generally resembles a slab of bacon. Salt pork is usually far saltier than bacon. Although it is no longer a staple of a sailor's diet, it has found a home in products like Boston baked beans.

Besides salt pork, other cured pork products include sugar-cured hams and bacon. For good reason, sugar-cured and honey-cured products have a much more desirable taste than salt pork. Almost all of the pig can be cured except for the pork loin. The pork loin is used to make pork chops, pork roasts, and spare-ribs. The cuts of meat that are used to make salt pork are high in fat content. The three cuts of the animal that are used to make salt pork are pork side, pork belly, and fatback.

Recipes

After looking at many formulations for curing different kinds of meat, it became apparent that most of the dry or brine recipes were very similar to this one. Several formulas for curing beef and pork allowed eight to ten pounds of salt for 100 pounds of meat. This formula could be adjusted to use brown sugar or cane sugar, depending on the product and taste you desire for your product. This formula could be mixed with sufficient water to dissolve the sugar and salt to make a brine solution. You could also reduce the amount of sugar for a brine cure to reduce the impact on the taste of the finished product.

Curing salt ....10 pounds

Sugar...3 ¾ pounds

Saltpeter..2 ½ ounces

Sodium nitrate ....½ to 1 ounce (excess nitrate is toxic)

PREPARATION INSTRUCTIONS FOR DRY CURE

1. After the ingredients have been mixed well, the curing compound will be rubbed on the pieces of meat. Remove excess fat from the pieces of meat, and be generous with the curing mix when rubbing it on the meat.

2. Place a layer of the curing compound on the bottom of your curing box.

3. Place the meat on the bottom layer of curing mix, then pack the curing mix all around the meat. If more than one piece of meat is

being cured, make sure a complete layer of mix is laid between the pieces of meat.

4. Many people have different opinions on how soon the meat needs to be unpacked and turned over, then repacked. The meat should be taken out no later than two days after the original packing. Then the bare spots need to be rubbed, the liquid brine drained, and the meat repacked. The meat should be fully cured after one week. The meat should remain refrigerated during this curing process. Experience gained over several curing events will enable you to refine the process to your preferences. Since the meat has not yet been cooked or hot smoked to kill microbes, the meat should remain refrigerated for safety.

INSTRUCTIONS FOR A BRINE CURE

1. To convert this formula to a brine cure, you will need up to five gallons of water.

2. Bring the water to a boil and stir in all ingredients except the meat.

3. After everything is dissolved, remove from heat and put in the refrigerator to cool down.

4. Find a suitable container such as a crock or plastic tub and put 1 to 2 inches of your solution in the bottom. You may need to start with more brine in the bottom of the tub if the pieces of meat you are working with are more than 2 inches thick.

5. Begin packing the meat in the tub or crock as close together as possible.

6. Pour in the rest of the liquid, making sure the meat is fully covered.

7. Put a lid on the container that ensures the meat will stay fully covered by the brining solution.

8. During the curing process, the meat needs to be in a place that will remain below 40 degrees Fahrenheit.

9.   After the meat is cured, rinse it off thoroughly. Dispose of the used brine. If you have more meat to cure, you will need to mix up a new batch of brine solution.

10. The meat is now ready for smoking. If you will use a hot smoke process, ensure the internal temperature of the meat reaches the correct safe cooking temperature for the type of meat you are working with. If you are cold smoking, remember cold smoking does not raise the meat to a safe cooking temperature, and the meat will have to be cooked before it is consumed.

SMOKED BACON AND OTHER CUTS

The initial process to smoke bacon begins with curing the meat. Home-cured bacon often has a saltier flavor than bacon purchased in the grocery store because the salt cure used to prepare the bacon is too strong. The key to achieving the flavor you desire is to find a curing formulation that is tailored to your specific taste.

Here are some general instructions for making smoked bacon at home:

1.   The best cut to use is the belly meat that comes from the area near the loin. The meat from the front area of the belly does not have as much meat because it is removed from the rib area. The meat from this area will have a much higher fat content.

2.   You should always use fresh cuts of meat that have been refrigerated to 42 degrees Fahrenheit for 24 hours prior to starting the curing process. The best meat will be come from an animal that has been slaughtered within the last day or so. If you went to a locker plant and purchased the meat, it should already be at the proper temperature.

3.   Cut your pork bellies to a shape that will allow you to cut slices of bacon after the product is finished. A slab of bacon is usually 1

inch to 2 inches thick. Slab bacon is rectangular in shape and can be purchased from many sources in 8- to 10-pound sizes. One pound of slab bacon, if sliced properly, can yield up to 35 slices. The idea is the same here; you need a finished product that is ready to use.

4. An effective brine formula was provided in the previous section. Use the formula that is provided, or one of your own. You can also find packaged brine solutions in stores that cater to home meat preservers. It is important to remember that a pork product like bacon is preserved through both the curing and the smoking. Smoking alone will not provide the protection against bacterial growth that curing in a brine solution provides. Smoking is designed to not only add to the preservation process, but also to add flavoring to the meat product.

5. To cure your pork, you will need a container such as a large crock or a tub made of plastic that will not break down under the influence of the salt in the brine. A wooden barrel designed for this purpose is also a great choice. Once you get your meat in the container, make sure the meat stays submerged in the brine. You may have to find a way to hold it down. The meat needs to stay in the brine at least four days under refrigeration. The meat should be rotated in the container every day.

6. Do your best to keep your refrigerator at a constant temperature of 38 degrees Fahrenheit. Lower temperatures will inhibit the curing process, and temperatures above 40 degrees Fahrenheit will not protect the meat from going bad.

7. After you are satisfied that the meat is sufficiently cured, take the meat out of the brine container and rinse it thoroughly with plenty of clean water. Paper towels are sanitary and provide the best means to dry the meat off after you have rinsed it. After the meat is dry, a thin skin called a pellicle will form on the meat. This skin will help

the meat absorb smoke better. The smoking process will not work properly if the meat is wet.

8. If you need more time to dry the meat, set a fan to blow over it. This process needs to be done as quickly as possible because at this point, your meat is not under refrigeration, and the only thing protecting your valuable product is the effectiveness of the cure. The pellicle will be identifiable as a gloss or sheen on the surface.

9. The next step is to hang the meat in your smoker. Make sure there is sufficient room between the pieces of meat for the smoke to circulate completely around all sides of each piece of meat. *A chart is provided in Chapter 1 on the different smoke flavors that are imparted by different species of wood.* At this point, it is time to fire up the smoker.

10. Since you are making bacon, you will probably cold smoke the meat; remember, it will take some time to get the results that you are looking for. Since cold smoking is done at temperatures between 80 degrees Fahrenheit and 100 degrees Fahrenheit, the meat will not be cooked and ready to eat. You may need to leave the meat in the smoker for up to eight hours.

11. When the meat is done in the smoker, it will need to be immediately refrigerated. Cold smoking does not cook the meat sufficiently alone to kill dangerous bacteria. Put it in the refrigerator to chill it down, and it will also be easier to slice. You can keep your homemade smoked bacon in the freezer without any loss of quality for at least three months.

MAKING PORK SAUSAGE

Sausage is a meat product made from a wide variety of ground meats. The primary sausage meats are pork and beef. Other meats that may be added to pork as extenders or flavor enhancers are chicken, turkey, goat, mutton, deer, and elk. Other necessary sausage ingredients are pork fat, salt, and herbs. Sausage casings were traditionally made from animal intestines that were carefully cleaned. Today, sausage casings are also made from proteins derived from beef or pig hides. Sausage casings can be removed before the product is consumed. As with other meats, sausage is preserved by curing, smoking, and drying.

General procedures for making sausage

To make sausage successfully, you must faithfully follow an established series of operations. Each step must be followed just exactly as it has been laid out, or else you will not come out with a product that really resembles what you started out to achieve.

The basic steps in making good sausage begin with the selection of quality meat. You cannot expect to make a good product if the meat you are using is of poor flavor, texture, and freshness. The meat will need to be ground up properly. You will need to pay close attention to the size of the grinding plate each recipe calls for. When it comes to mixing the meat, spices, and cures, you are going to get your hands dirty. The best way to mix up some of the recipes is just to dig in with your hands and mix it all up. Next, the product will need to be stuffed into casings and then put in the smoker. If you do all of these operations properly, you will have a wholesome and tasty product that you can be proud of.

When you begin selecting the meat you will use, not only are you looking for freshness, but you will also want to consider the percentage of fat. Many of the recipes you will see indicate what percentage of fat the meat you are using should have. A quality that is more difficult to determine is the ability to bind with all of the ingredients and hold the shape that you are seeking in a good sausage. Fresh meat should not be spoiled, contaminated, or show evidence of bacterial growth. You are looking for meat that is of equal quality to any other meat you would use in your kitchen. Always use the best quality spices, herbs, and seasonings you can find. These are the elements of sausage that bring out the wonderful tastes you desire in a good meat product.

The curative agents are the most misunderstood part of the process of making sausage for many people. The great misconception is that meat that has been exposed to a strong curing formula is somehow preserved permanently and will not spoil. Although meat cannot be preserved without a curing agent, cure does not mean that all of the other steps in the process can be shortchanged. Almost everyone understands that salt and sugar are part of a good cure recipe, but most people do not understand the importance of sodium nitrite. Sodium nitrite, when used properly, will inhibit the deadly toxin that comes from the microorganism *Clostridium botulinum* from growing in your sausage. Sodium nitrite does help to develop the cured color you are looking for in a meat product, and it also helps to develop that very desirable flavor that people expect in their sausage. If you use a commercially produced cure, be sure to follow the directions on the label.

At all times, you must be mindful of the temperature of the meat during the phases of making sausage. Any time the temperature of the meat gets above 40 degrees Fahrenheit, bacterial growth will begin immediately. If there will be significant amounts of time between operations when the meat will be sitting on the counter, put the meat in the refrigerator until you are ready for it. Always do what it takes to maintain as cool a temperature as possible during all the grinding and mixing operations. You will always grind sausage meat twice and mix every ingredient thoroughly.

The spices and other ingredients in a particular recipe will be mixed into a slurry that usually uses around two cups of water. Water dissolves the salt and cure and makes mixing easier, helping all of the different flavors and tastes to develop.

The second grinding of the product will bring your mixture to the consistency called for in the recipe. Before the second grinding, you will have thoroughly mixed the slurry with the meat. After the second grinding, all of the ingredients and meat will be the same size, making for an easier product to eat. If you do not have the luxury of owning a grinder, do not despair. You can always purchase quality ground meats that will work.

If you are making a fresh breakfast sausage, you will not need to stuff your product into a casing. Fresh sausage can be left in a bulk form and fashioned into patties when you are ready to cook and serve it. On the other hand, most types of sausage will be formed into some kind of shape by forcing it into a casing and heating it in a smoker.

Casings are like all other foods in that they need to be preserved to ward off dangerous microorganisms. If the casings you are planning to use have been preserved in salt, they will need to be soaked in lukewarm water for a period of at least 30 minutes before you will be able to use them effectively. After the casings have been soaked and the salt has loosened up, you will need to flush the casings with cold, clear water. It will also be necessary to run the water through the center of each casing. All of this detailed work is necessary to remove the extra salt the casings were packaged with. If you have some unused casings, they should be drained and recovered with salt and put in the freezer.

Fibrous casings are used for products requiring a lot of strength, such as summer sausage. Fibrous casings also are available in a greater variety of sizes. They also allow moisture to flow out of the product and smoke to get into the meat. They can be removed from the meat product very easily. They should be soaked in 80 to 100 degrees Fahrenheit water for at least 30 minutes prior to use. The casings may be punctured with the point of a knife to eliminate air and fat pockets in the finished product.

Collagen casings have many of the same characteristics as those that are found in natural and fibrous casings. They were developed for use with fresh pork sausage and pepperoni sticks. The uniformity of size and strength make them an ideal choice for the home sausage maker. Collagen casings are also permeable, and they will shrink tightly around the meat.

The smoking process is designed to use controlled heat to pasteurize the meat and extend the shelf life as long as possible. Smoking also gives the meat a smoky flavor and makes the appearance more palatable. The heat that develops in the smoking process causes the meat to take on an expected color and brings about the changes in the proteins in the meat that enables the sausage to hold the desired shape when the casing is removed.

Recipes

Bill's summer sausage

This recipe was provided courtesy of Bill Tomaszewski of Tin Man Meats.

INGREDIENTS

Meat...100 pounds (70 percent venison/ 30 percent pork butt)

Note: A doe with a field-dressed weight of 100 pounds should yield about 25 pounds of meat, and a buck with a field-dressed weight of 165 pounds should yield about 60 pounds of meat. Given these ratios, this recipe as written may require more than one deer to finish the product. You will need to do a little math and cut the ingredients down according to the amount of venison you actually have.

Summer sausage seasoning mix.........Use a premixed sausage mix labeled for 100 pounds of meat

Pink curing salt ....4 ounces

Sausage casings................................50

Special note: Please check all package instructions when mixing ingredients. Product labels and instructions may vary.

EQUIPMENT NEEDED

- Two-quart pitcher
- Sausage stuffer
- Meat Grinder
- Smokehouse
- Woods such as hickory, wild cherry, apple, or pecan

PREPARATION INSTRUCTIONS

1. Make sure all the meat has been chilled. Double-grind all the meat though a ³⁄₁₆-inch grinder plate. Meat is placed into a container. Seasoning and cure is mixed in with water. The amount of water you use will depend on the package instructions for the brand of summer sausage seasoning mix you are using.

2. The meat is then stuffed into the casings and hung in the smokehouse for 24 hours to let the cure and seasoning blend throughout the meat. The next day, the meat is heated to 100 degrees to eliminate sweating. The heat removes some of the excess moisture from the product. Then smoke is applied.

3. The smokehouse temperature is maintained at 163 degrees until the meat hits a completion temperature of 152, usually in 14 to 16 hours.

4. The finished summer sausages are then placed in a cooler of cold water to release the heat and prevent shrinkage. This is called "showering."

5. Afterward, the sausage is hung on sticks in a cool place for seven to ten days to reach the desired texture and color. This is called "blooming."

6. Either wrap the sausage with freezer paper, or vacuum-seal it and place it in freezer. Use the sausage wrapped in freezer paper first. Vacuum-sealed sausage is for long-term storage.

Notes: 2 ¼- by 20-inch casings are used instead of 3-inch casings because these do not take as long to smoke. *There are references for the equipment and supplies mentioned in the recipe in the Appendix.*

Sweet Italian sausage

This recipe was provided courtesy of North Dakota State University and Julie Garden-Robinson.

INGREDIENTS

Note: 70 percent lean meat will cook down significantly. You can find frozen pork trim for sale in 60 pound packages. A local butcher shop is the best place to find this product. If you have a smaller quantity of meat than this recipe calls for, simply divide all the ingredients to the appropriate ratios. For example, you could easily divide all the ingredients in half.

Pork trim (70 percent lean) ....90 pounds

Water ....3 quarts

Salt..3 cups

Sugar...1 cup

Cure ....6 tablespoons

Cracked fennel seed ....7 tablespoons plus 3 teaspoons

Paprika ....3 ounces

Black pepper ....⅓ cup

Cayenne pepper ....⅓ cup

Garlic powder ....⅓ cup

Oregano ....2 tablespoons

Sweet basil ....1 tablespoon

PREPARATION INSTRUCTIONS

1.   Coarse-grind the pork trims.

2.   Add salt, water, sugar, cure, and spices.

3.   Regrind through ¼-inch diameter plate and stuff into pork casings.

4.   As this is a fresh sausage, no smoking is necessary. This product could be hot smoked if you choose, however.

5.   Refrigerate until you are ready to cook it.

6.   Product must be cooked before serving.

Lar's Super Garlic Sausage

This recipe was provided courtesy of North Dakota State University Extension and Julie Garden-Robinson

INGREDIENTS

Pork trim (50/50) ....33 pounds

Beef or venison trim ....17 pounds

Tender Quick ....1 ½ cups

Salt ....⅔ cup

Brown sugar ....1 cup

Black pepper ....½ cup

Garlic powder...................................6 tablespoons

Sage..2 teaspoons

Allspice..1 teaspoon

Coriander...1 tablespoon

Warm water.......................................1 gallon

PREPARATION INSTRUCTIONS

1.   Grind the meat through a coarse plate.

2.   Mix the spices in water and pour over meat; mix thoroughly.

3.   Grind through a coarse plate again and stuff in hog casings.

4.   Using a cool smoke at 90 degrees, smoke for 12 hours.

5.   Product must be cooked before serving.

Note: If you do not like garlic flavor, cut back on that spice. This product would also work well with a fine grind if you prefer a finer sausage product.

SAFETY ISSUES WHEN PRESERVING PORK

It is very important to follow heating requirements when cooking pork for your family. Pork must be heated to an internal temperature of 160 degrees Fahrenheit to ensure that disease-causing parasites are destroyed. Humans are susceptible to a parasite named Trichinella Spiralis. Trichinosis is contracted from eating undercooked pork. Pork producers are working very hard to reduce the trichinosis in hogs fed with grain. Pork is completely safe for human consumption if it is heated to at least 160 degrees Fahrenheit.

There are a number of microorganisms that can be a problem with ham that is not prepared and stored properly. Trichinella and Staphylococcus are dangerous microorganisms that can grow quickly in ham that is not cooked and refrigerated properly. Ham must always be cooked sufficiently to kill trichinae. *Staphylococcus aureus* is a microorganism that is able to survive high levels of exposure to salt. As soon as the ham is sliced, this microorganism will grow on the surfaces that have low-salt concentrations. All sliced ham should be returned to the refrigerator just as soon as you have all the slices you need. Hams are also susceptible to the growth of molds on exposed surfaces. The key to the protection of your family and friends is to keep all pork products properly refrigerated and not left out on the counter for extended periods of time, especially in hot weather. When you cook a pork product, make sure you get the internal cooking temperature up to the recommended level.

This smoked pork will make a great meal with a side of baked beans.

CASE STUDY:
THE TIN MAN SMOKEHOUSE

Bill Tomaszewski
Saint Peters, Missouri
Tin Man Meats

Bill Tomaszewski built this smokehouse out of materials he already had in his garage and some items he purchased at a local hardware store. The smoker uses a wood stove like the one that some people still use to heat their homes. The wood stove is connected to the meat-smoking chamber by stovepipe. Smoke flows from the wood stove into the smoking chamber. The flow of smoke to the cooking chamber is controlled by the air valve on the stove and the flue, or smokestack, that comes out of the back of the stove. The arrangement efficiently provides sufficient smoke and heat to the meat in the chamber to bring meat products to a safe internal cooking temperature.

Tomaszewski built the smokehouse that he and his family use to preserve a variety of meats such as summer sausage, flavored meat sticks, fish, pork, and poultry. Cure is added to prevent spoilage because low heat is used. Smoke emits a number of acids, which cling to meat and form an outside layer of skin. The acid performs a role in preserving meat by preventing the growth of surface mold and bacteria.

When his wife Kay first saw the shiny beginnings of the smoker in the back of the truck, she was reminded of the movie *Twister* because of the tornado-tracking device. As she watched Bill put the smoker together, it quickly became obvious that he had a plan in mind. Although the smoker does not look like one that you could purchase on the retail market, it serves his family's purposes very well.

The more the smokehouse took shape, and as soon as the flue was placed on the top and the support legs underneath, it was obvious to Kay that this was now the Tin Man from *The Wizard of Oz*. Ever since, she has labeled all of their packages with this name.

This smoker is a wonderful example of what a person can do with a little ingenuity and some knowledge of the science of smoking meat. A smoker like this will last for many years. When you build your own equipment, you will know exactly how it works and how to make any adjustments that become necessary. It will be easier to make repairs on a smoker you have built in the backyard verses a piece of equipment that was purchased in a store.

Here is a picture of the Tin Man smokehouse.

Image provided courtesy of Bill and Kay Tomaszewski.

CHAPTER 6:
Preserving Lamb and Mutton

Mutton is not consumed as much in North America as it is in the rest of the world. There are many different opinions why this is so. Some believe the lack of desire for mutton is a lingering dislike for sheep that started in the late 1800s as a feud developed between cattlemen and sheep men. Cattlemen claimed that sheep ruined pasturelands because sheep crop the grass too close to the surface, causing the grass to die, thus ruining good grazing land. Although this attitude is not based on sound scientific information, it had enough influence to discourage farmers and ranchers from getting involved in the sheep industry. Agricultural scientists have shown that grazing sheep and cattle on the same rangeland can be effective using sound management principles. Sheep prefer immature grasses and weeds. In fact, sheep will eat weeds that are a problem for cattle, thereby improving the pastureland for cattle. Cattle prefer mature grasses, so the two foragers can use the same rangeland and complement each other.

Another reason cited for our nation's lack of interest in mutton stems from the World War II experiences of servicemen being fed large amounts of canned mutton. Mutton was a cheap food source for a nation trying to finance the feeding of millions of servicemen and women around the world during the war. Many people feel that servicemen returning from the war were tired of eating mutton, so the market for the meat dried up.

A third reason cited for a lack of interest in mutton is that past U.S. government subsidies for wool made it much more profitable to use sheep to produce wool than meat. Because of the need to keep sheep strictly for wool production, there was no longer a ready availability of the meat. According to this viewpoint, a whole new generation of people has grown up with little or no contact with mutton.

Regardless of the reason, you should feel free to try new recipes and new kinds of meat.

With the rapidly changing demographics in America, the consumption of mutton may become a much more mainstream product than it is today. Mutton is not always easy to find in the grocery store, but it is a meat option that can provide an excellent change of pace at the dinner table. In many countries, mutton is the primary meat source, and many wonderful recipes are coming to the United States as people migrate to this country from all over the world.

MUTTON: SOMETHING DIFFERENT FOR SUPPER

There is a difference between the meat that is called lamb and the meat that is called mutton. Lamb comes from animals that are less than one year old, usually six to eight months. Mutton is therefore from sheep at least one year old. Mutton is said to have a texture that is softer than lamb but a flavor that is stronger. The issue of tenderness has some controversy because it is easy to understand how a properly raised lamb will have meat that would be considered very tender. The flavor is influenced by the forage the animals feed on. Sheep being raised primarily on grasses from pastureland or Western rangeland will produce meat with a different flavor and fat content than animals raised on prepared feeds in a feedlot.

Another issue to consider is where the recipe that is being used originated. In places such as Asia and India, people use the term "mutton" to describe the meat from both sheep and goats. This is an important thing to understand since recipes from those parts of the world may be using the meat from the two animals interchangeably. Goat meat (chevon) is definitely different from meat from a sheep (mutton). *Good recipes and instructions for the use of chevon are discussed in Chapter 7 of this book.*

Some people claim that mutton and chevon have the same taste as venison or veal. Much of the taste issue revolves around the feed the animals eat. Sheep will consume weeds found on rangelands that may influence the taste of meat if the weeds are the primary feed the animal consumes. Eating an occasional weed is not going to have a major affect on the taste of the meat.

When the taste of lamb or mutton is compared to venison, there are some facts to consider. Hunters will affirm that there is a much different taste to venison between an animal that has been feeding in the corn fields of Nebraska and an animal that is feeding in Western rangelands where there is sparse vegetation of short grasses, sage brush, and pinion pines.

What this whole discussion boils down to is that you should ask questions of the butcher when selecting a new cut of meat for the first time. It may be important how the animal was raised when taste is considered. Some people prefer beef that was raised naturally on a ranch and was never in a feedlot, while others people prefer grain-feed beef, which has a greater percentage of marbling. However, most of the cattle in North America are fed in feedlots for their last 120 days before going to the slaughterhouse.

During the time cattle are in a feedlot, they will be fed a variety of grains, with corn being the primary feed source. Corn-fed beef will be highly marbled with a smoother, consistent flavoring. Marbling is the small flecks of fat that can be seen throughout the cut of meat. The higher amount of marbling a cut of beef has, the higher grade it will receive. The higher grading is warranted because well-marbled beef is considered to be more tender and juicy.

The same level of selectivity can be applied to lamb, mutton, or any other meat you are trying for the first time. The following list of cuts from a lamb will help you to know what to look for when selecting this meat for the first time.

Cuts of lamb

1. Neck
2. Scrag (from the upper neck area)
3. Best end neck cutlets
4. Middle neck
5. Best end of neck
6. Loin
7. Loin Chops
8. Saddle (comes from the loin)
9. Chump chops (comes from the hip area)
10. Leg (comes from the rear leg)
11. Shoulder

BEST WAY TO FREEZE MUTTON

As the chapter develops, there will be more information provided on the preparation and preservation of lamb. Since lamb is more readily available in the grocery store than mutton, most of the available recipes focus on lamb. Most of the information that will be provided in this chapter can be used to prepare either lamb or mutton.

Lamb and mutton may be frozen in their original packaging. For long-term storage, the package of lamb should be placed in an airtight freezer bag to protect the product from freezer burn. If you know in advance that the meat will be put in the freezer for long-term storage, you can take it out of the original package before it is initially frozen and placed in a freezer bag or other container intended to protect meat in the freezer. Instructions on freezing lamb and mutton are the same. Lamb may be refrozen after it has been cooked. Thawed-out lamb should be consumed within three to five days. Lamb cuts and ground lamb can be stored in the freezer for up to nine months, while cooked lamb can be safely stored in the freezer for up to three months.

CANNING, CURING, AND SMOKING OF LAMB AND MUTTON

Much of the information, instructions, and recipes for other types of meat can be adapted to the preparation of lamb and mutton. As compared to other meat products, lamb is considered a lean meat; that is, it has low levels of marbling. The fat on lamb is around the edges of each cut of meat, so it can be trimmed off easily. As you adjust the many recipes in the book to use with lamb or mutton, make the adjustment as you would any other lean meat.

Canning lamb

The process for canning lamb is the same as you would use to can other types of meat. The meat must be trimmed of excess fat. The meat can be put into the canning jars cooked or uncooked, but in either case, meat must be processed in a pressure canner following the time and pressure requirements that have been established by the USDA. To reduce confusion, some steps for safely canning meat are provided in the following list:

1. Meat must always be processed in a pressure canner according to established procedures to ensure your finished product is safe to eat.

2. Always use canning jars to process meat because they are manufactured to stronger standards than jars used for mayonnaise and other commercially processed food.

3. It is best to remove as much fat and gristle as possible. Excessive fat interferes with the canning process, and gristle left in the meat will negatively affect the quality of the finished product. The next step is to remove as much white muscle covering as possible.

4. When filling canning jars with meat you must be careful to ensure fat and grease does not build up on the lip of the jar. Fat and grease on the lip may impede the lid making a good seal.

5. Pack the meat loosely in clean, hot canning jars, leaving 1 inch of headspace below the lid. It will be easier to pack the meat if you use wide-mouth jars. Remember: do not pack the meat tightly in the jar. If the meat is packed too tightly the meat may not cook thoroughly. Add salt at this time unless you plan to salt the meat at the time that it is served. Consider using ½ teaspoon for pint jars, and 1 teaspoon for quart jars.

6. Before placing lids on the jars be sure the lip of the jars are clean and dry to facilitate the sealing process. Place lids on jars and screw on securing rings.

7. Place jars in the pressure canner ensuring that jars do not touch each other. Fill canner with water to the level prescribed by the instructions for your canner. Process the meat for the time and pressure prescribed for your elevation.

Curing lamb and mutton

Curing any type of meat involves the addition of either some form of salt, nitrates, or sugar product. The purpose for curing meat may be to preserve the product for use without refrigeration for a period of time, or to simply add flavoring. To ensure that dangerous bacteria in meats are effectively inhibited, make the brine solution with a salt concentration of at least 15 percent. This concentration level will inhibit all but a few rare bacteria. Cooking the meat to the proper internal heat level is the best way to ensure that all dangerous bacteria are destroyed. A safe curing brine solution would consist of 2 cups of salt and 2 cups of sugar mixed thoroughly into 1 gallon of water.

Although the curing and brining of lamb and mutton is not necessarily a common practice if the purpose is for long-term preservation, common curing and brining practices will work just as with other meats. Lamb and mutton are more commonly exposed to curing processes for the purpose of adding flavoring. Additionally, a great reason to cure lamb or mutton will be to use a smoked lamb recipe like the one that follows this section.

Smoking lamb

Lamb and mutton are very important in Iceland. From the beginning of the nation, the raising of sheep has been one of the primary agricultural products of this isolated island nation. The Icelandic people work very hard throughout the year to make a living, so holidays are very important to them. Christmas Eve is a very special day, so many businesses and shops close at noon on that day. At 6 p.m., church bells begin to ring, signaling the start of the Christmas holiday. The majority of Icelandic families will serve smoked lamb on either Christmas Eve or Christmas day. Eating smoked lamb is a very important holiday tradition for the people of Iceland.

There are many other places in the world where the consumption of lamb is an essential part of the diet. Because of the worldwide popularity of lamb and mutton, there is a wealth of resources for wonderful recipes that you and your family would really enjoy. In this country, wool production is the main focus of the sheep industry; so it is sometimes a challenge to find fresh lamb in the grocery store or the meat market. Meat from a mature sheep will have a much stronger taste than that of a lamb. If you do not have any experience preparing and eating lamb, it is recommended that you do some research and explore the excellent recipes that can be found for lamb.

Recipes

Lamb canning recipe

1. Remove excess fat.
2. Remove large bones and cut meat into desired pieces.
3. If canning raw meat (raw pack), fill jars, leave 1 inch of headspace, and do not add liquid.

4.   If canning hot meat (hot pack), precook meat until rare by broiling, boiling, or frying. Pack hot meat loosely in clean hot canning jars.

5.   Cover hot meat with boiling broth, water, or tomato juice, leaving 1 inch of headspace.

6.   Install lids and rings and set in pressure canner, ensuring that jars are not touching each other.

7.   At 2,000 feet, process at 11 pounds of pressure; process pint jars for 75 minutes and quart jars for 90 minutes.

Altitude Adjustment Chart for Lamb Using Pressure Canner with a Dial Gauge

Altitude	Pressure
2,001 to 4,000 ft	12 pounds
4,001 to 6,000 ft	13 pounds
6,001 to 8,000 ft	14 pounds

Smoked leg of lamb

*This recipe is provided courtesy of the Smoke Ring (**www.thesmokering.com**).*

INGREDIENTS

Boneless leg of lamb ....5 to 6 pounds

Cloves of garlic ....6 to 9

Olive oil ....1 to 2 cups

Salt ....Enough to rub on entire area of the meat

Pepper ....Enough to rub on entire area of the meat

PREPARATION

1.   Chop cloves of garlic and mix in a bowl with olive oil.

2. Rub mixture all over the meat, making sure the surface is completely covered.

3. Season all sides of the meat with salt and pepper, according to taste. It is also suggested that you rub it in.

COOKING INSTRUCTIONS

1. Start charcoal in grill and push it to one side, since this will be an indirect cooking process.

2. Add a chunk of hickory wood to the charcoal to add some additional smoke flavor.

3. Put an aluminum pan next to the charcoal to catch the meat drippings.

4. Put the lamb on the grill fat side up, above the drip pan, and opposite the coals. Put grill cover on.

5. Monitor internal meat temperature and the temperature inside the grill. Temperature inside the grill should be 325 to 350 degrees Fahrenheit.

6. Lamb should cook for about two hours and reach an internal temperature of 150 degrees Fahrenheit. At this point, the meat is done.

7. Slice the lamb into ¼-inch slices for serving.

8. The reserved drippings can also be used to make gravy. Heat the drippings, add salt to taste, and add a teaspoon of sugar. Add cornstarch to thicken. Serve with the lamb.

ALTERNATE SLOW-SMOKING INSTRUCTIONS

1. Rub the lamb with the garlic and olive oil per the previous recipe instructions.

2.   Cover the meat with salt and pepper per the previous recipe instructions.

3.   Place lamb in shallow dish or non-aluminum pan and cover. Place in refrigerator and chill for six to eight hours.

4.   Start smoker, and use hickory wood chips to create smoke. It may be best to soak wood chips in water prior to placing them in the smoker.

5.   After smoker is up and running, place the meat on a low rack and smoke for six to seven hours, or until the internal temperature of the meat reaches 150 degrees Fahrenheit.

6.   During the smoking procedure, maintain a constant temperature in the smoker of 170 to 180 degrees Fahrenheit. If the smoker temperature is allowed to rise above 185 degrees Fahrenheit, the meat will overcook, dry out, and shrink.

7.   If you have a commercially purchased smoker, follow the particular instructions that come with the equipment.

Dried lamb

The recipe was adopted from a recipe provided courtesy of North Dakota State University Extension and Julie Garden-Robinson.

INGREDIENTS

		RECIPE CUT IN ONE FOURTH
Lamb	100 pounds	25 pounds
Salt	9 cups	2 ¼ cups
Sugar	6 ¾ cups	1 ¾ cups
Nitrate	3 ½ tablespoons	1 tablespoon

PREPARATION INSTRUCTIONS

1. Using 1 ½ ounces per pound of meat, rub the salt, sugar, and nitrate mixture onto the lamb, making sure all areas are well covered.

2. Rub the lamb twice at three to five day intervals. Keep refrigerated until cure is complete.

3. Allow two days per pound of meat for the cure to complete. This may also be calculated by using seven days of curing time per inch of thickness of the cut.

4. After the lamb is cured, rinse it with cold water several times; then hang it and allow it to dry for 24 hours.

5. Apply a light or heavy smoke as desired. The level of smoke flavor will be determined by the amount of time the meat is exposed to the smoke.

6. Hang in a dry, well-ventilated room for further drying.

7. Use the largest pieces of lean meat you can find.

Note: If you prefer to have a cooked product, smoke and cook to an internal temperature of at least 160 degrees Fahrenheit.

SAFETY ISSUES WHEN PRESERVING MUTTON

You can safely cook lamb without defrosting using an oven or stovetop, and even on the grill, but it may take up to 50 percent longer to bring the meat to a safe cooked temperature. On the other hand, frozen lamb cuts must never be cooked in a slow cooker or an electric crock-pot because the outer surface of the meat will be overcooked before the internal temperature of the meat reaches a safe cooking temperature. Lamb needs to reach a temperature of 150 degrees Fahrenheit to be safe for human consumption.

CHAPTER 7:
Have Some Goat for Supper

More people in the world eat goat meat more than any other kind of meat. It is estimated that there are over 450 million goats in the world. Of that number, it is estimated that less than 10 percent of the worldwide goat population lives in North America. The majority of goats are raised in the Middle East and Asia. The small size of goats and wide range of acceptable feed sources make them the ideal choice for people with small farms and limited resources. The proper name for the meat of goats is chevon, but few people know it by that name. In some parts of the Middle East and Asia, goat meat is called mutton.

With the rapidly changing population demographic in the United States, and with people immigrating from regions where goats are the main meat source, the production of goats is growing very rapidly, making chevon more readily available. Many negative stereotypes Americans hold concerning the consumption of chevon are slowly changing as people become more informed about the nutritional value of the meat.

In addition to meat, goats provide milk for people to drink and hides for use as clothing. Goats are willing to eat weeds that other animals ignore and are useful for clearing fields of unwanted plant growth. For this reason, people using goats for milk production must be careful about what the goats in a dairy herd consume. The weeds and other things that goats feed on can have a direct impact of the quality of milk they produce. With careful feeding, goat milk is very healthy and has a wonderful taste. Some infants that cannot tolerate cow's milk can sustain on goat's milk, which will taste much like cow's milk.

Goat production is also important to people seeking to develop a more independent lifestyle. Goats allow farmers with small land plots that cannot sustain larger animals to increase their productivity.

Chevon is a healthy alternative meat option that has a distinctive flavor that will seem very different to people who primarily consume beef. It will not seem too different to people who consume wild game meat such as venison, however. Some people believe that venison and veal have a taste that is similar to chevon. According to the International Kiko Goat Association, "Chevon is lower in cholesterol than rabbit, venison, or beef. The saturated fat in cooked goat meat is 40 percent less than that of chicken, even with the skin removed. It is 50 to 60 percent lower in fat than similarly prepared beef, but has the same or more protein content."

GOAT BREEDS THAT ARE USED FOR MEAT PRODUCTION

Goat meat comes from several breeds found in the United States. This list contains some goats that have traditionally been considered dairy goats only. In order to keep dairy goats producing milk, they must get pregnant and produce kids.

1. **French Alpine, Oberhasli, Saanen**, and **Toggenburg** are breeds developed for milk production in the mountains and valleys of the Alps. They have short and erect ears, with faces that are straight or

dished and color patterns that are very distinct. Alpine dams — or mother goats — produce a good quantity of milk, and they usually produce big kids. Alpine kids will usually become lean with long legs as they mature.

2. **LaMancha** is a breed that was developed in the United States by cross-breeding many different breeds of goats from Europe. They have tiny earflaps, making them look like they do not have any ears at all. LaMancha and Nubian dams usually produce a smaller quantity of milk, and they produce kids with lower weights at birth. An advantage for the meat producer is that these goats usually have greater weight carcasses when they get older. All animals do not grow according to breed expectations. Many factors such as available feed and quality of care provided will make a difference in any breed. When it comes time for you to select a goat to slaughter for meat, look more to the qualities of the individual animal than at its breed.

3. **Anglo-Nubians (Nubians)** were developed and bred by crossing British, Middle Eastern, and Indian breeds. These goats have distinctive "roman" (convex) noses, with long and dangling ears.

The following strains or breeds of goats have been genetically bred specifically to produce a superior meat goat. Not all of the following types of goats are actually separate breeds, but they do pass on to their offspring distinct characteristics that may eventually gain recognition as a distinct breed.

4. **Spanish meat goats** have descended from goats that arrived in the United States with settlers from Europe. Goats that escaped from farmers migrated to the south, interbreeding with goats that came to the New World with Spanish colonists. These goats are a mixture of many breeds and strains. Because of the way they had to live in the

wilderness, foraging for food wherever they could find it and fighting off predators on their own, they have become a very hardy goat. They are not the largest of goat varieties. Farmers and ranchers used the largest goats to breed for better size and meat production. Other breeds have been used to improve milk and meat production characteristics.

5. **Tennessee meat goat** is a somewhat different strain of goat that appeared on a farm in Tennessee in 1880. A farmer realized he had a flock of goats with muscles that "locked up" when they were frightened. Myotonic is a word that describes a condition in which muscles lock up when an animal is startled. The condition can be so strong that sometimes the goats will actually fall over. This is the origin of the Tennessee fainting goat breed. Ranchers in Texas selected animals from this population with the largest bone structure and the heaviest muscles to use as breeding stock. By this method, a goat has been developed that is a good meat-producing animal. The action of stiffening and relaxing of the animals' legs develops greater muscles, tender meat, and a higher ratio of meat to bone.

6. **South African Boer goat** is a result of goats from the Bantu tribes in Africa being bred with European and Asian goats brought to Africa by Dutch colonists and immigrants. During the 1800s, South African farmers began the process of breeding goats with the characteristics of superior growth rates, high meat to bone ratio, excellent fertility rates, and distinctive color patterns. This breed has the distinction of a white body color and a red head. Since 1959, these goats have been recognized as a distinct breed. Boer goats began coming to the United States in the early part of the 1990s. Boer goats have become a major factor in the United States meat goat market.

7. **New Zealand Kiko goat** was developed in New Zealand when farmers took feral does with better meat characteristics and bred them with Saanen and Nubian bucks in an effort to increase milk production with greater butterfat percentages. The goats with offspring that showed the greatest potential for superior weight gain became the basis of the development of the breed. The ears of Kiko goats look like the ears on Spanish goats, and the Kiko goats have larger bodies. This breed tends to be white.

HOW TO PREPARE CHEVON FOR THE FREEZER

After any type of meat is frozen, it is best to keep the meat at a constant temperature of around 0 degrees Fahrenheit. Freezing does not necessarily destroy all of the microorganisms that can cause disease, but it inhibits the growth of these dangerous microbes and bacteria. Bacteria begin to grow when meat is stored in the danger zone of 40 to 140 degrees. Meat still has to be properly cooked after it is thawed out in a safe manner to ensure that no one will get sick eating what has been prepared.

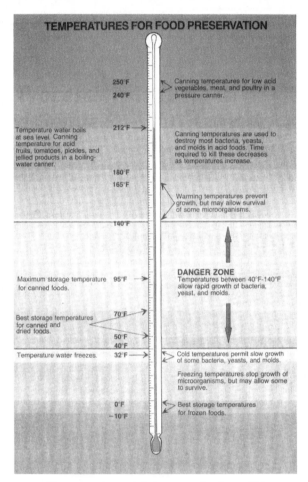

Temperature is especially important for chevon. This illustration shows general temperature guidelines for food preservation. Image courtesy of the USDA.

CANNING, CURING, AND SMOKING CHEVON

As a general rule, canning procedures will be the same as for lamb and mutton. There are some special considerations to be aware of when preparing and serving chevon.

1. When you bring fresh goat meat home from the market, it should be packaged in an air- and moisture-free freezer container before long-term storage in the freezer. Properly packaged goat meat can be kept frozen for six to nine months.

2. If you cook chevon using too high of a heat setting, the meat will lose its moisture and become tough. You should always slow down the cooking pace for best results.

3. Fresh chevon should always be kept in the coldest section of your refrigerator. Another good place to store uncooked fresh chevon is in the meat compartment in your refrigerator. Fresh, uncooked meat that is stored at the coldest possible temperature should be OK in the refrigerator for about one week.

4. Chevon that has been cooked or smoked must be chilled down as quickly as possible to preserve that fresh and tender taste you are looking for.

Recipes

Making and canning ratatouille

*This recipe was provided courtesy of David G. Blackburn of **www.canningusa.com**.*

Ratatouille is a stewed vegetable dish that works well with a wide variety of meats. The recipe for canning ratatouille is included here because it would work very well with chevon as an accompanying dish.

INGREDIENTS

Olive oil ....¼ cup

Garlic clove, diced (optional)...1

Medium onion, halved and then sliced........................1

Medium eggplant, unpeeled, cubed one inch 1

Medium zucchini, unpeeled, cubed one inch...............1

Medium tomatoes, coarsely chopped, or you may

substitute whole tomatoes ....2 medium

or 1 ½ cups

Herbs de Provence...¼ cup

Salt (more or less to taste)...½ teaspoon

Pepper (more or less to taste) ....½ teaspoon

Lemon juice, for canning only....................................2 tablespoons

PREPARATION INSTRUCTIONS

1. Only use perfect vegetables.

2. Wash and prepare ingredients.

3. Sauté garlic and onion in olive oil for approximately five minutes.

4. Add all other ingredients (except lemon juice for canning), and sauté on low heat for 20 minutes or until eggplant is tender, gently stirring every five minutes or so.

5. If canning, mix in lemon juice.

6. If canning, use raw or hot-pack method with 1 inch of headspace in the canning jar.

7. Process with a pressure canner for 90 minutes at 11 pounds, or 10 pounds with a weighted gauge.

8. *For elevations above 1,000 feet, adjust cooking time according to the altitude and time adjustment chart provided in Chapter 2.*

9. After processing, remove the jars and place on a towel separated by at least 1 inch to cool and seal naturally.

Chevon summer sausage

This recipe was adapted from one provided courtesy of North Dakota State University Extension and Julie Garden-Robinson. It was originally formulated for use with venison but would work just as well with goat meat.

INGREDIENTS

Goat	15 pounds
Pork trimming 50/50	10 pounds
Salt	⅔ cup
Cure	1 ½ tablespoons
Mustard seed	2 ½ tablespoons
Black pepper	½ cup
Sugar	½ cup
Marjoram	1 tablespoon
Monosodium glutamate (optional)	1 tablespoon
Garlic powder	3 tablespoons

PREPARATION INSTRUCTIONS

1. Mix salt and cure with a coarsely ground product.

2. Pack in a shallow pan and place in cooler for three to five days.

3. Mix in remainder of spices, regrind, and stuff in 3-inch fibrous casings.

4. Smoke at 140 degrees Fahrenheit for two hours; raise the temperature to 160 degrees Fahrenheit for two hours.

5. Finish the product at 170 degrees Fahrenheit until the internal temperature reaches 155 degrees Fahrenheit.

6. This recipe was presented here using goat meat, but it could be used with any red meat.

CASE STUDY: MEAT PRESERVATION FROM THE PAST

Eugene W. Oster and Katie Blum Oster Born in Germany in 1875, migrated to the United States in 1902

This account came from an interview with a gentleman who has a memory of butchering and processing goats at his home property prior to 1944, when he went into the Navy during World War II. Eugene Oster and his mother, Katie, would butcher the goats and make the meat into sausage by hand with no modern equipment. Eugene Oster's father, Jakob, did not participate in the butchering and sausage making after Eugene became old enough to help his mother. Some of the sausage-making techniques that will be described in this case study should not be used anymore because of the difficulty in cleaning intestinal materials at home for human consumption.

On butchering day, the process began by selecting an animal for slaughter and leading it out into the yard. They selected young animals that would not be raised and used for breeding purposes. Then Eugene and his mother would lay the goat in a wheelbarrow so the goat's head was hanging over the edge. Katie had a superstition that if the goat bleated while it was lying in the wheelbarrow, she would stop the process and try the next day. She would not butcher until she had an animal that submitted to handling without making any noise.

As soon as they got an animal, they could begin butchering. Eugene would cut the neck and allow the animal to bleed on the ground. A slit would be cut just above the rear hooves between the tendons, and a small pole would be inserted through the legs to keep them spread apart. The goat would be taken to a place where the goat could be hung up so the head was about 2 feet off the ground. This process had to be done quickly because the goat would skin out easier while it still retained some of its body heat.

Next, they would cut the hide down the inside of the rear legs down to the pelvis area, being careful not to cut any of the urinary tract or fecal area. All

skinning should be done with a very sharp skinning knife that is laid between the fingers. The next step would be to remove the hide from the
rear legs, doing their best not to cut through the hide and get hair on the
meat. Then they would to pull down on the hide that was around the legs
and cut around the pelvis area, again being careful not to cut any of the
urinary and fecal organs and tubes. It helped to reach back around and
loosen the hide around the tail. Eugene said they skinned the tail to keep
hair out of the meat. If the urinary tract or fecal organs were cut open and
the contents spilled on the meat, the entire carcass had to be disposed of
because the meat would be ruined.

Next, with the skinning knife between the fingers, they would cut a slit in
the hide down the stomach without cutting into the actual stomach. If the
stomach was cut, there would be a terrible smell to deal with. If you are
going to save the hide for later use, it is best to avoid cutting through the
hide. Eugene said that he had to keep the skinned-back hide tight in his
left hand so that he could easily remove the hide without cutting into the
stomach or through the hide. At this point, they would skin all around the
animal, eventually pulling the hide down around the animal's neck. They
would get a hold of the urinary and fecal organs and cut through the membrane holding the internal organs in the body cavity. The best thing would
be if all the internal organs would come out in one piece. The organs
would be put in a tub. If someone wanted to use the liver and the heart,
there was still the need to keep the urinary tract organs off to the side until
they could be separated and disposed of. They carefully cut the heart and
liver out of the internal organ sack and removed all bloody veins and con-
necting parts. Eugene would remove the intestines from the body organs
by cutting as close to the stomach as he could without exposing the stomach contents. Then he would empty all of the contents out of the intestines
and begin flushing them out. The intestine would be used as their sausage
casing. Eugene said it would take up to two hours to completely flush and
clean the intestine for sausage making.

The next step would be to get both hands on the esophagus and give a
hard jerk and pull it out of the animal. Then they would cut the head off
and finish removing the hide and set it aside for later preservation. They
would hang the animal to cool in a place where the family cat or other
pests could not get to it. The next day they would begin the butchering.

Katie needed two grinders to get the sausage done efficiently. The goat was cut into quarters and brought into the kitchen to be deboned. The deboned meat was run through the first grinder at a course setting, and the ground meat put in a tub. All of the meat was mixed together with the spices Katie used to make her sausage. Eugene could only remember that his mother used some sage, salt, and pepper. To Eugene's knowledge, Katie never used sugar or any other curative agent.

The meat was then run through a grinder with a finer setting. The length of intestine was put over the outlet of the grinder and filled to the length that was desired. At the point where the intestine was cut, they used butcher string to tie off the end. Since they did not have a freezer, they took the meat to the local locker plant to have it frozen and stored for a small monthly fee. Eugene said that if they started butchering early in the morning, they would have time to get the sausage to the locker plant before it closed in the evening.

The author and publisher of this book do not recommend using the intestines from the animal you slaughtered to make your sausage anymore. There are plenty of meat-processing businesses today to purchase safe and sanitary sausage casings from. You can also purchase pre-mixed sausage seasoning and curing mixes that will help you to make a product you can be proud of.

SAFETY ISSUES WHEN PRESERVING CHEVON

Consumers are advised to always wash their hands in warm soapy water before and after handling any raw meat. Ground chevon must be heated to 160 degrees to ensure it is safe for human consumption. Large cuts of chevon can be safely cooked to an internal temperature of at least 145 degrees as measured with a meat thermometer.

CHAPTER 8:
Preserving Good, Lean Bison Meat

The consumption of buffalo has been very important in North America for centuries. Many American Indian cultures placed great dependence on the millions of buffalo that once roamed the continent. In recent years, buffalo consumption has had resurgence, with many ranches breeding and selling buffalo as a lean alternative to beef. According to The National Bison Association, consumer demand for bison has risen recently. *The Vail Daily* reported in 2010 that "Rocky Mountain Natural Meats had an increase in annual sales from two million pounds in 2003 to eight million pounds in 2009."

The recipes presented in this chapter should provide encouragement to return to this traditional food source. Remember that many of the other recipes throughout the book can also be used with bison meat. All you need to do is to consider how lean the meat is, and make the necessary cooking adjustment.

MUCH LIKE BEEF, ONLY LEANER

Bison meat has about one third of the fat of beef. The lower fat content of bison makes it cook quicker and dry out faster under intense heat. People cooking bison need to pay close attention to how fast the meat is cooking to ensure they do not overcook or prematurely dry out the meat.

Freezing tips for bison

- It is best to keep the meat in its original package until it is to be used. It is safe to freeze the product in the package the meat came in for periods of less than two months. Meat processors do an excellent job of packaging meat, whether they use clear cellophane or some form of meat packaging paper.

- Hunters should use packaging products that are specifically designed for protecting meat products in the freezer. *There are several resources for freezer storage containers presented in the Appendix.*

- If you plan to store the meat for more than two months, you will need to put the package of meat in a larger freezer bag, removing excess air.

- Ground meat and smaller pieces will store safely in the freezer for up to four months.

- Larger cuts will safely store for six to nine months.

HINTS FOR CANNING BUFFALO

Canning buffalo will follow much the same procedures as canning other red meat. Just remember that buffalo or bison meat will be much leaner than beef. During the canning process, be sure to keep your meat chilled, and do not let it sit out on the counter too long before you either precook it or put it in your canner and start the canning process. Meat must remain refrigerated or preserved in some manner to inhibit bacterial growth.

Since buffalo meat is naturally leaner than beef, it may produce less natural juice when it is being cooked. Recipes that are adapted for cooking buffalo need to be adjusted to add a little more cooking liquid. The fact that buffalo is a leaner meat means that it is well suited to the canning process because there will be less fat in the meat solution to interfere with the final cooking and jar sealing process. *There is a canning recipe in Chapter 9 under "Canning big game" that will also work well with buffalo.*

Recipes

The original recipe called for ground beef, but it will work just fine with buffalo meat.

Marinara sauce recipe

*This recipe was adapted from **www.canningusa.com** courtesy of David G. Blackburn.*

This is an easy-to-can recipe that would make a wonderful dinner for your family and friends who drop in on short notice. In reality, two recipes are provided here: one for canning, and one for you to prepare as part of your regular meal planning.

INGREDIENTS

	DINNER	CANNING
Tomatoes	1 quart	8 quarts
Onions	2 medium	16 pounds
Carrots	2	16
Red or green bell pepper	1	8
Garlic	1 clove	8 cloves
Ground beef (bison)	1 pound	8 pounds
Red wine vinegar	2 tablespoons	1 cup

Olive oil ....1 tablespoon   ¼ cup

Salt..2 teaspoons   4 tablespoons

Pepper ....1 teaspoon   2 tablespoons

Lemon juice ....For canning only ¾ cup

PREPARATION INSTRUCTIONS

1. Blanch, peel, and chop tomatoes.

2. Dice garlic and carrots, and chop onion and peppers.

3. Sauté onions, peppers, and carrots in the olive oil until the onions are translucent.

4. Add ground meat and continue to stir.

5. When the meat begins to brown, add the crushed garlic.

6. Cook for about five minutes before adding the chopped tomatoes.

7. Simmer for two hours, stirring occasionally until sauce begins to thicken.

8. Add vinegar, salt, and pepper to taste. You may continue simmering for thicker sauce if desired.

9. Add lemon juice for canning.

10. Can using hot-pack method with 1 inch of headspace.

11. Process with a pressure canner 60 minutes for pints or 70 minutes for quarts, with pressure at 11 pounds, or 10 pounds for a weighted gauge.

12. *For elevations above the 1,000-foot level, see the time and pressure adjustment chart in Chapter 2.*

13. After processing, remove from boiling water and place jars on a towel, separated by 1 inch, to cool naturally as quickly as possible.

14. Label jars and place in storage.

CURING, SMOKING, AND MAKING JERKY

Since buffalo is so much leaner than other red meats, curing, smoking, and jerky formulations will need to be adjusted to account for quicker drying times. The absorption of salt will be different when the bison is exposed to a salt brine solution.

Recipes

Beef jerky

This recipe was provided courtesy of Julie Garden-Robinson and North Dakota State University Extension.

INGREDIENTS

Lean beef (buffalo)	5 pounds
Salt	1½ tablespoons
Black pepper	1 tablespoon
Cardamon	1½ teaspoons
Marjoram	2 teaspoons
Cure (pink color)	1½ teaspoons
Monosodium glutamate	2 teaspoons
Cayenne pepper	2 teaspoons
Garlic powder	1 tablespoon
Liquid smoke	½ cup
Water	½ cup

PREPARATION INSTRUCTIONS

1. Mix all spices together with meat.

2. Mix well until meat is tacky.

3.   Grind and press into a loaf pan lined with foil.

4.   Put in cooler or freezer to firm product for slicing.

5.   Slice as thin as desirable.

6.   Spray oven racks with oil, and then lay slices on the racks.

7.   Spray with liquid smoke and garlic mixture.

8.   Dry in oven at 170 degrees Fahrenheit for two to three hours.

9.   If you use a dehydrator, follow the instructions that came with your dehydrator.

Note: Temperature is very important in the making of jerky. The USDA Meat and Poultry Hotline's current recommendation for making jerky is to heat the meat to 160 degrees Fahrenheit before the dehydrating process to assure that any bacteria present will be destroyed by wet heat.

CASE STUDY: MAKING SAUSAGE

North Dakota State University Extension
Julie Garden-Robinson, PhD, Food and Nutrition Specialist
Martin Marchello, PhD, Professor, Animal and Range Sciences

Sausages are made from beef, veal, pork, lamb, poultry, and wild game, or from any combination of these meats. Sausages can be classified in a variety of ways, but probably the most useful is by how they are processed. Processing methods give sausages easily recognizable characteristics.

EQUIPMENT

It only requires a grinder, a good meat thermometer, and some general household items to make excellent sausage. If you do not have a grinder, you can purchase ground meat from the store. Many products do not need to be smoked, but liquid smoke can be added to give the smoky flavor desired, or you may add a small portion of a cooked, smoked product like bacon to produce the smoky flavor.

You can purchase a household smoker or make one. An old refrigerator converted to a smokehouse works quite well if you need to smoke the product. Smokehouses can be as simple as a tarp covering or as sophisticated as a commercial unit.

PROCEDURE

Sausage making is a continuous sequence of events. Each step in the proper sequence is important to a successful operation.

It is not practical to consider each step separately or to assign more importance to one phase or operation, but for convenience and illustration, we can break sausage production down to four basic processes: selecting ingredients, grinding and mixing, stuffing, and thermal processing.

SELECTING INGREDIENTS

Meat should be fresh, of a high quality, have the proper lean-to-fat ratio, and have good binding qualities. The meat should be clean and not contaminated with bacteria or other microorganisms. In other words, meat used in sausage production should be as safe as any meat you would prepare in your kitchen. Selecting spices and seasonings and combining them in proper amounts is important. They must complement each other to create a satisfying taste.

Cure, an essential part of some formulations, is sodium nitrite (usually 6 percent) on a salt base. It usually can be purchased at a local locker plant. Sodium nitrite is necessary to inhibit production and growth of the deadly toxin produced by the microorganism *Clostridium botulinum*. It also gives the characteristic cured color to a sausage product and improves flavor. Commercial products such as Freeze-Em-Pickle, Tender Quick, and saltpeter can be found in markets and at drugstores. If these are used, be sure to follow directions on the packages.

GRINDING AND MIXING

For safety, keep the temperature of the meat as cold as possible during grinding and mixing. The usual procedure is to grind the various meats coarsely and then add the rest of the ingredients, mixing thoroughly.

Slurry is made of the spices and salt using two cups of water. Water is added to dissolve the curing ingredients, to facilitate the mixing, and to give the products their characteristic texture and taste.

The product is then ground again to the desired consistency. Mixing should be done before the final grind. Grinding improves the uniformity of the product by distributing the ingredients and making the particles the same size. Unless you have special equipment, it is desirable to work with small batches (up to 25 pounds), as the cure and seasoning can be more evenly distributed. If you do not have a grinder, buy ground meats, add the seasonings, and mix thoroughly by hand.

STUFFING

It is not necessary to stuff fresh sausage meat. It can be left in bulk form or made into patties. Most sausage, however, is made by placing the ground ingredients in some type of forming device to give them shape and hold them together for thermal processing. The casing materials may be natural or manufactured. Natural casings include the gastrointestinal tracts of cattle, sheep, and hogs. Generally, hog casings are the most suitable for home use and work quite will for Polish and breakfast-type sausages. They are digestible and are very permeable to moisture and smoke.

All casings preserved in salt must be soaked in lukewarm water for at least 30 minutes before use. Flush each casing under cold water, running cold water through the casing. This removes excess salt from the casing. Unused casings can be drained, covered with salt, and frozen.

Fibrous casings are more suitable for summer sausage and similar products because of their greater strength and the variety of sizes available. They are permeable to smoke and moisture and can easily be removed from the finished product. These casings should be soaked before use in 80 to 100 degrees Fahrenheit water for at least 30 minutes, but not more than four hours before use. If the casings are not pre-stuck, they should be punctured with a knife point or pin to eliminate air and fat pockets in the finished sausage.

Collagen casings contain the attributes of both natural and fibrous casings. They have been developed primarily for use in products such as fresh pork sausage and pepperoni sticks. They are uniform in size, relatively strong, and easy to handle. These casings also are used for the manufacture of dry sausages, because they are permeable and will shrink.

For cooked products that are generally water-cooked (like Braunschweiger), plastic casings impermeable to water are used.

THERMAL PROCESSING

Sausage is smoked and heated in order to pasteurize it and extend its shelf life, as well as to impart a smoky flavor and improve its appearance. Smoking and heating also fixes the color and causes protein to move to the surface of the sausage so it will hold its shape when the casing is removed.

A few products, such as mettwurst, are smoked with a minimum of heating and are designed to be cooked at the time of consumption. Others, such as liver sausage, are cooked but not smoked.

Procedure for smoking polish sausage: After stuffing in hog casings (pre-flushed), let hang and dry. Smoke at 120 degrees Fahrenheit for one hour, 150 degrees for one more hour, then at 170 degrees for two hours or until an internal temperature of 141 degrees Fahrenheit is reached. Remove from smokehouse and spray with hot water for 15 to 30 seconds. Follow with cold shower or dip in a slush tank until internal temperature reaches 100 degrees Fahrenheit. Let dry for one to two hours. Place in a cooler.

Procedure for smoking summer sausage: After stuffing in casing, smoke at 140 degrees for one hour, 160 for one more hour, then at 180 for two hours or until the internal temperatures reach 155 degrees Fahrenheit. Remove from the smokehouse and follow the same procedure as for polish sausage.

Procedure for making cooked sausage: After stuffing the ground ingredients into an impermeable casing, put the sausage into a pan of water. Heat water to 170 degrees and hold it there until the sausage reaches 155 degrees. A thermometer is essential for obtaining proper temperature. The water should not boil, as this will ruin the product. If you are making a sausage product using cooked meat, be sure the meat was cooked with low heat.

SAFETY ISSUES WHEN PRESERVING BISON

The recommended safe internal cooking temperature is 155 degrees Fahrenheit. There are some people who prefer to prepare their meat to the rare heat level, but you must be sure to get the internal temperature of the meat high enough to kill dangerous bacteria. Cooking bison meat rare brings the temperature to about 135 degrees. Great caution should be taken when heating meat for human consumption 20 degrees below the recommended safe temperature.

CHAPTER 9:
Preserving Game Birds and Big Game Animals

The subject of game birds encompasses a wide range of meat options. This chapter will address the preparation and preservation of waterfowl and all kinds of upland game, like wild turkey, American woodcock, ring-necked pheasant, bobwhite quail, ruffled grouse, and sharp-tailed grouse.

Part of the enjoyment of hunting game birds is being able to prepare and eat the rewards of the hunt. When properly preserved, game birds can be enjoyed for many months after the hunt. Game bird hunting is a valued tradition. The fees that hunters pay for licenses across the country fund most of the wildlife conservation efforts in each state that have preserved the wonderful wild places people enjoy with their families. Because of money paid for hunting and fishing licenses, many species of animals that were hunted to near extinction have recovered from the numbers that were present on the North American continent at the beginning of the 20th century.

Hunting is one of the greatest family traditions in America. Many big game animals share characteristics with beef, chevon, and mutton. American Indians and early American pioneers depended on the meat of wild animals that had been butchered and preserved. This chapter will endeavor to celebrate the traditions of the past and at the same provide people with the information they need to be able to continue harvesting game and safely preparing it for human consumption.

Big Game Animals in North America that are Hunted for Meat

See the listings provided in the Appendix from across North America for information on hunting big game animals.

Bears: Bears are hunted for meat and their hides. The main precaution is to cook the meat sufficiently to ensure that the parasite that causes trichinosis is killed. Hunting bears is a considerable undertaking and should not be considered without seeking the assistance of a knowledgeable guide.

Moose: The meat is very similar to other red meats with a distinctive rich flavor, but it is much leaner. The head of a large bull moose makes a great trophy in the den. Moose is most plentiful in Alaska, but it may also be hunted in some remote areas of the lower 48 states.

Alligator: The meat is lean and considered to be very flavorful. Because of their life in the water, they are susceptible to accumulating mercury in their fatty areas, so special precautions must be taken to remove fatty areas before the meat is consumed. Alligator hides make very good leather that is used in many apparel items.

Caribou: The meat is very lean, and it is considered a very healthy meat alternative. There is a large herd in Alaska that is estimated to contain over 500,000 animals. Caribou has been a major part of the diet of native Alaskan people for several centuries.

Bighorn sheep: Bighorn sheep are hunted primarily for their value as a trophy animal, but the meat is very nutritious and flavorful. Since the numbers of bighorn sheep are limited, hunting this animal would be considered the experience of a lifetime.

Bison: At one time, these animals numbered in the millions across the Western plains of North America. By the early 1900s, they had been hunted to the brink of extinction. Due to the hard work of many people, these wonderful animals have been brought back to sufficient numbers to have hunting seasons in some areas of the West. The meat presents a high-value alternative to beef that is very lean and nutritious. There are several farming and ranching operations in the Western states that concentrate on the production of Bison meat products.

Cougar: Although limited seasons do exist in some Western states, these animals would be hunted primarily as a trophy animal. The old-time mountain men of the early 1800s are said to have preferred the meat from a cougar above any other animal they could have killed for meat. People who have eaten cougar consider it similar in taste to pork. This meat must also be well-prepared to protect from the parasite that causes trichinosis.

Mountain goat: Due to the rigors of the life they live in the wilderness, the meat from mature animals will tend to be tougher than if you can harvest a younger animal. The mountain goat is also hunted primarily as a trophy animal. For most people interested in hunting, a mountain goat hunt would also be considered a great opportunity.

Deer: There are many different species of deer across the United States. Deer are hunted in almost every state, and they provide an important food source for many people. Deer meat is known as venison. People have many different views on the quality of the meat. Deer that are harvested from Western areas where the primary food sources are rough grasses, pinion nuts, and scrub oak will have a much different taste than animals that feed on corn fields in the Midwest.

Musk ox: There are significant efforts being undertaken to restore the numbers of this majestic animal. Musk oxen were traditionally valued for the wool they produce and as a source of meat. There are still opportunities in Alaska to go on a hunt for one of these animals.

Antelope: The meat is considered to have a gamey taste. To make the meat easier to work with, it should be soaked in milk. The use of seasonings is important when preparing the meat. Antelope is one of the greatest hunting experiences you can have. Success depends on your long-range shooting skills.

Elk: A cow elk will provide up to 200 pounds of meat, and a mature bull will provide several hundred pounds more. There are several different subspecies of elk in the United States, and all of them provide an excellent hunting experience. Bringing a large bull elk out of a remote area of a national forest can present a significant challenge that you should not attempt without help. A mature bull elk can also produce a fabulous trophy to hang on your wall.

CASE STUDY: PRESERVING MEAT FROM HARVEST TO STORAGE

Bill and Kay Tomaszewski
Saint Peters, Missouri
Tin Man Meats

Bill Tomaszewski has been in the field of meat preservation since 1979. His wife, Kay, joined in 1998. He is able to properly preserve meat starting at the time it is harvested through the processing and storage phases. From the field to the table, venison is his specialty.

The Tomaszewski family harvests venison, fish, quail, pheasant, and turkey with gun, archery, and fishing techniques. The pork butt and hamburger they use is from the market to be added to the venison for some of the sausage recipes. Their meals are very diverse; they are able to enjoy fish one night and turkey the next. Prices fluctuate on meats in the grocery stores, so they have the benefit of having different meats available, no matter what their budget may be. For example, if they want steak fajitas, they are able to substitute the deer meat that has been frozen for grocery-bought beef and not make a decision based on the price of steak at the store.

The preservation of venison begins in the field immediately after the animal is harvested because fresh meat is vulnerable to bacteria. Spoilage organisms need moisture and warmth for development, so the body cavity needs to be opened up to release body heat. The animal is transferred to an area where the meat can be quartered and stored at a temperature between 34 to 38 degrees. Bill hangs a deer in the outdoors until it can be quartered only if the temperature is less than 40 degrees. They are very particular to ensure the meat is washed and free of hide and hair because organisms can be transferred from the hide of the animal and even from their hands and the tools they use to butcher. The meat is kept cool until the time it is processed or used for cooking to prevent spoilage. They make a variety of fresh sausage, including Bratwurst, Knockwurst, Boudin, Italian, and Chorizo. To preserve the meat, it is ground, then seasoned and stuffed into casings, vacuum-sealed, and frozen for later use. Fresh sausage is not cured because it is cooked at a high temperature and either refrigerated immediately after cooking or consumed just as soon as it is prepared. The high cooking temperature that is used to prepare fresh sausage eliminates the chance of food poisoning.

They also grind and package venison for burgers. Other meats harvested from the animal (deer steaks, loins, and roasts) are sealed and frozen, and they have a dehydrator to make deer jerky. They use the same rules with fish. Preservation starts by putting the fish on ice or in a live well until cleaned and refrigerated or frozen until use. They also soak fish in a brine solution before smoking to preserve it. The most important rule of meat preservation is to keep the meat cold until is time to cook.

The Tomaszewski family understands that food preservation is the prevention of spoilage and bacteria, so they follow proper sanitation habits. The equipment is washed thoroughly after use with hot water and soap and left to cool and dry before storage to prevent bacteria from growing and breeding. All the spices and cures are kept in tightly sealed containers when not in use. Microorganisms cannot be destroyed completely, but over the years they have practiced good sanitation habits so their meat does not spoil. It is recommended that room temperature should not be more than 70 degrees Fahrenheit. The room is free of flies, pests, and their pets; just one fly can ruin thousands of dollars of meat. Flies and rodents carry many bacteria that can be harmful to humans. The presence of even one fly or mouse would be a matter of concern in any food processing facility. Gloves are always used. Hand washing is important, especially after using the restroom. Hairnets are recommended as hair contains a large amount of bacteria. They use plastic cutting boards now because hardwood boards have been shown to breed bacteria. Plastic cutting boards can be effectively cleaned many times over and only need to be replaced when they have become worn out from use.

Meat is kept between 34 to 38 degrees Fahrenheit to slow the process of deterioration. Fresh meat is most vulnerable at the time of processing, so they make sure that all the supplies are ready and available before actually taking the meat out. Depending on what they are processing, the finished product may be vacuum-sealed or wrapped and put back in the refrigerator, freezer, or prepared for smoking. When using cure as a preservative, it is very important to maintain a specific meat temperature. If the temperature is less than 34 degrees, the curing process should stop, and if it goes above 40, it will cause the meat to begin spoiling. It is also important to monitor temperatures when smoking meat. The temperature required for sausages and other meats is 152 degrees. They use a dual thermostat to monitor the inside temperature of the meat and the inside temperature of the smokehouse.

They use cures in all of their smoked products and use different types of cures depending on the meat that is being processed. *(A chart showing different kinds of curative agents is included at the end of this case study.)* There is a saying: "If it can't be cured, don't smoke it." For hundreds of years, nitrate has been used as a cure because it has the ability to give the meat special flavors and protect against botulism. These bacteria spores are found in every type of meat and are harmless, but under favorable conditions can produce a deadly toxin. The presence of oxygen, low acidity, moisture, proper nutrients, and temperatures in the range of 40 to 140 degrees is when the conditions are perfect for food poisoning unless you use a cure.

Smoking meat is a slow process. They monitor the meat temperature in the smokehouse closely with the dual thermostat that also features an alarm. The meat temperature has to reach 152 degrees, but the smokehouse temperature should not go more than 165 degrees or else the fat, used as a binder, turns to oil and seeps to the outside of the casing. This causes the meat to crumble. A temperature sway in either direction may set up the right conditions for food poisoning or failure of the finished product.

The Tomaszewskis' products cannot be found in a store or restaurant, yet they are distinct and delicious. They know their ingredients are fresh and preserved properly to prevent spoilage. It is less expensive to preserve and process the meat themselves versus buying at the market. In their family, meat preservation and processing has been passed down through generations. Their grandfather would say, "Don't kill it unless you're going to eat it." The love of hunting and fishing also comes with the responsibility of using the meat that is harvested and not wasting. They encourage meat preservation for the self-satisfaction of knowing the food is prepared right and a variety of food is available for long-term use. If someone they know shows interest in learning, then they offer assistance in getting started or let them observe their meat processing.

Curative Agents

Agent	Functions
Salt	• Flavor enhancer • Antimicrobial • Facilitates cure working throughout the meat
Sugar	• Flavor enhancer • Balances the effects of the salt cure • Provides energy to fuel necessary bacterial change for curing
Nitrite	• Inhibits discoloration of food products, inhibits the development of botulism, and has a pink color
Nitrate	• Used to destroy microorganisms in food products that cause human illness; occurs naturally in leafy green vegetables

Salt and nitrates are used with most meats that are being cured; sugar cure specifically is used with pork products, such as ham, or poultry products, such as turkey.

FREEZING GAME BIRDS

The quality and texture of the finished product depends on proper meat handling procedures with the slaughter, field dressing, cooling out period, and preparation in your kitchen. The first important step in maintaining a safe and healthful wild game meat product is to ensure that fecal contaminants never come in contact with the meat. If at all possible when handling wild game, wash or sanitize your hands often so that contaminants are not unconsciously transferred from one part of the animal to another.

The best way to preserve the fresh quality of the meat you have harvested in the field is to get it into the freezer just as soon as possible. The meat should be thoroughly cleaned and then wrapped in a freezer container or freezer wrap, while being sure to remove as much air and moisture as possible. If stored properly, most wild game meat will keep for up to a year without a significant loss of quality.

If you are going to slice or butcher your meat in any way before it is frozen, it will be important to follow the safe meat-handling and kitchen sanitation rules that were covered in Chapter 2 and other sections of the book. An important kitchen sanitation consideration that has not previously been covered is the cleaning of wooden cutting boards. Wooden cutting boards can present a real danger of spreading contamination if not cleaned properly. They should be washed and scrubbed thoroughly after each use with a non-toxic cleaner and a stiff nylon brush. Then you should rinse the board completely with a solution that will sanitize it, such as a chlorine bleach solution. Do not fill a pan with sanitizing solution and submerge the board, as the sanitizing solution will be absorbed into the cutting board.

After you have cooled out and cleaned the birds you have brought home, remove excess fat, as it will quickly turn rancid. It is best not to stuff your game birds before you freeze them because bacteria can grow quickly when it comes time to defrost the bird. The stuffing will thaw out sooner than the bird and be subject to bacterial growth. Commercial meat producers have special procedures to safely prepare pre-stuffed poultry. Remove all of the entrails before putting birds in the freezer. Cool the bird to 40 degrees Fahrenheit as soon as possible before cooking or putting the bird in the freezer to inhibit the growth of microorganisms, as well as to keep ice crystals from forming to protect the meat from freezer burn. You can cool meat down to 40 degrees Fahrenheit by placing it in the refrigerator.

PUTTING GAME BIRDS IN JARS

Canning procedures for game birds will be much the same as domestic poultry. Some of the important information from the previous section on canning poultry found in Chapter 4 has been included here for your benefit. It is always best to use the freshest birds possible. If game birds have been freshly slaughtered and dressed, it is best to set them in the refrigerator to chill for six to 12 hours before canning. Large birds provide better flavor after they are removed from the jar.

Cut the bird into sizes that will fit into the size of jar you are planning to use, either pints or quarts. Game birds may be canned with or without the bones, and they can be hot packed or raw packed. If you choose to use the hot-pack method, precook by boiling, steaming, or baking until the bird is two-thirds of the way done. Add up to 1 teaspoon of salt per quart jar if desired. Fill the jars with pieces and hot broth from the cooking process, leaving 1 ¼-inch of headspace. Install lids and bands and place in pressure canner.

If you choose the raw-pack method, add 1 teaspoon of salt per quart jar if desired, and loosely pack in the jar. Do not add liquid when raw packing the meat. Always leave 1 ¼-inch of headspace in the jar. Install lids and bands and place in pressure canner.

Follow the chart provided with your pressure canner that lists the time and pressure food should be processed at for your elevation, or you can refer to the following chart. If you have a recipe for a particular kind of game bird that provides different information on pressure cooking, follow your recipe, or if there are special instructions that came with your pressure cooker canner, follow those instructions.

Processing Chart for a Dial Gauge Pressure Canner

	Jar Size	Processing Time	0 to 2,000 ft	2,001 to 4,000 ft	4,001 to 6,000 ft	6,001 to 8,000 ft
Bones in Meat Hot and Raw	Pint	75 min.	11 lb	12 lb	13 lb	14 lb
	Quart	90 min.	11 lb	12 lb	13 lb	14 lb
No Bones Hot and Raw	Pint	65 min.	11 lb	12 lb	13 lb	14 lb
	Quart	75 min.	11 lb	12 lb	13 lb	14 lb

Processing Chart for a Weighted Gauge Pressure Canner

	Jar Size	Processing Time	0 to 1,000 ft	above 1,000 ft
Bones in Meat Hot and Raw	Pint	75 min.	10 lb	15 lb
	Quart	90 min.	10 lb	15 lb
No Bones Hot and Raw	Pint	65 min.	10 lb	15 lb
	Quart	65 min.	10 lb	15 lb

Recipes

Canning Game Birds and Onions

This recipe was adapted from a recipe from **www.canningusa.com** *courtesy of David G. Blackburn.*

INGREDIENTS (MAKES 4 QUARTS)

Game bird cut into pieces.................8 pounds

Onions peeled and sliced..................8 pounds (equal to weight of meat)

Salt..1 tablespoon (or to taste)

Pepper...1 tablespoon (or to taste)

Olive oil ....⅛ cup

COOKING INSTRUCTIONS

1. Brown meat in a skillet using olive oil on medium heat for approximately five minutes per side. Add salt and pepper. If making a large quantity, brown some meat in an additional skillet. After browning, combine the two in the pot.

2. Add onions (a large pot will be needed); cover and cook at a simmer for 1 ½ hours or until onions are caramelized. It may be advantageous to debone birds and remove the skin.

3. For canning, use the hot-pack method with 1 inch of headspace in the jars.

4. Process with a pressure canner for 75 minutes at 11 pounds of pressure or 10 pounds for a weighted gauge.

5. *For elevations above 1,000 feet, use the time and pressure adjustment chart provided in Chapter 2.*

Note: If the strong flavor of onions is unappetizing to you and your family, you may consider reducing the amount of onions you include in the recipe, or use a sweet onion variety such as Valencia for a less powerful onion taste.

CURING AND SMOKING GAME BIRDS

Game birds will be prepared for curing in much the same way as other types of meat. All of the same food safety rules apply to freshly slaughtered game birds. Until poultry is cooked to at least 165 degrees, it may contain dangerous bacteria. Curing does not cook meat, so remember the poultry will still need to be heated to the proper temperature before it is consumed. Hot smoking techniques can raise the internal temperature of the meat to the safe level. It is important to remember that game birds may be leaner than the chicken that you purchased at the grocery store. When cooking leaner meats, you may not naturally have sufficient juices from the fat to keep the meat from burning and scorching, so you may need to add some cooking oil.

Recipes

General-purpose brining solution

GENERAL BRINING TIPS

When working with brining formulations, you cannot assume that 1 cup of one kind of salt will equal 1 cup of another kind of salt. One cup of table salt weighs approximately 10 ounces. If a recipe calls for 1 cup of table salt and you want to substitute a different type of salt, weigh out 10 ounces of the salt you want to substitute and you should be OK. Salt comes in many different types and brands, such as sea salt, canning and pickling salt, and kosher salt, which may have different specific brand titles.

INGREDIENTS

Water ....One quart

Kosher salt.....................................¼ cup (an equivalent amount of sea salt will add a different flavoring)

Sugar...½ cup (using brown sugar could provide a different flavor enhancement)

Note: If you need a greater volume of brine, simply multiply these ingredients by two or by four, for example.

PREPARATION INSTRUCTIONS

1. Mix all of the ingredients together in a container large enough for your total brine volume. A plastic or ceramic container will work. A container that would be reactive to salt would not work.

2. For safety's sake, home-brining operations should not exceed 2 gallons of solution.

3. For a single 1-pound piece of meat, one hour in the brining solution should be sufficient.

4. If you have a real thick piece of meat, you may need to use a brine injector and inject the brine into the thickest part of the meat.

5. Regardless of the weight of the meat or the level of brine effect that you desire, it should not be necessary to leave meat in brine solution for more than eight hours.

6. Refrigerate the meat during brining or keep the process below 40 degrees Fahrenheit. Make sure the meat remains completely submerged throughout the entire process.

7. After the meat is removed from the brine, discard the brine solution. Once the brine has been used, the curing agents have been exhausted, and you do not want to take the chance of cross-contaminating your next meat product.

8. Immediately after the meat is removed from the brine, either begin the smoking process or refrigerate the meat until it will be used.

PREPARING BIG GAME MEAT FOR THE FREEZER

The meat from large game animals such as deer, elk, or bighorn sheep should be handled the same as you would handle any other meat. In the case of an animal you have shot, make sure you clean up the area around the bullet wound and any related meat that was damaged by the entry of the bullet. You can cut the meat up yourself and package it, or take it to the local meat processing plant, also known as a locker plant, due to the fact that they rent freezer lockers for you to store your meat. The key is to make sure that you follow all of the safe food handling procedures that have been discussed throughout the book.

Here is a short review of simple meat freezing tips that were presented earlier. All of these recommendations can be used with any type of meat you are going to put in the freezer.

- Cut the meat into portion sizes that will feed your family for one meal when the package comes out of the freezer. This will help reduce the chances for waste.

- Use packaging that is designed for use in the freezer. Freezer bags are made of thicker material than sandwich bags and will resist tearing to provide protection from freezer burn. Plastic freezer containers are also designed to protect frozen foods from freezer burn and from the absorption of excess moisture that accumulates when the freezer door is opened and the temperature in the freezer rises.

- Do your best to remove all the air from freezer bags. Air that remains in the freezer bag will contribute to frozen food drying out and going stale.

- Make sure the package is sealed completely to reduce chances for freezer burn. Freezer burn causes discoloration of the surface of the meat. Although freezer burn does not make the product inedible, it does give meat an unappetizing appearance. The discoloration is an indication that the meat has absorbed excess moisture and has been affected by the temperature fluctuations of the opening and closing of the freezer door. Removing unnecessary moisture reduces the chance for ice crystals to form over long-term storage.

- Be sure to label packages to eliminate the chances of losing track of what you have in the freezer. Labels help you use food before it reaches its safe storage life.

HOW TO CAN BIG GAME

Some foods naturally inhibit bacterial growth because the food product has a high acid content. Meat is a low-acid food, so all meats that are not refrigerated or preserved in some manner are highly susceptible to bacterial growth. Canning processes need to heat meat to 240 degrees Fahrenheit to ensure that all dangerous microorganisms are destroyed. This can only be accomplished in a pressure canner.

Most big game meat is naturally leaner than beef and will produce less juice during any cooking process, so recipes that are adapted for cooking big game meats need to add a little more cooking liquid. On the other hand, leaner meats are well suited to the canning process because there will be less fat in the meat solution to interfere with the final cooking and jar sealing process.

Normal meat canning procedures that you would use for any other meat will also apply to wild game. It is best to have your meat fully chilled before you begin the canning process. Well-chilled meat will resist bacterial growth during the time you are handling it in preparation for canning. Meat that has a naturally strong flavor can be soaked for one hour in a brine solution, which can be 1 tablespoon of salt mixed with 1 quart of water. Large bones should be removed before cooking since they will not fit into a canning jar.

If you have the time, you can remove even the smaller bones. If you leave the small bones in your product, they will make a good treat for your dog later on when your family enjoys the meat from the jar.

Recipes

Basic canning recipe

1. If you are going to use quart jars, estimate using 3 to 4 pounds of fresh meat per jar and half of that for pint jars.

2. Remove all excess fat and gristle from the meat, along with the white muscle covering, and cut into 1-inch cubes, cutting across the grain of meat. If you are using wide-mouthed canning jars, it is okay to cut the meat into larger pieces as long as the meat is not packed into the jars so tightly that the meat will not cook thoroughly.

3. For the hot-pack method, the meat can be precooked by either roasting it or browning in a skillet. It is okay to add a small amount of fat or oil during the precooking if your meat is very lean.

4. For the hot-pack method, pack meat loosely in the canning jars, and add 1 teaspoon of salt to each jar you fill, or to your taste. Along with the pieces of meat, include at this time any boiling broth or meat drippings you have from the precooking process. Add sufficient water or tomato juice if you prefer to finish filling the canning jar, while leaving 1 inch of headspace.

5. For the raw-pack method, it is not necessary to add liquid to the meat when it is packed in the canning jars. The meat will produce its own juice during the time in the pressure canner. Pack the meat loosely in the canning jars, leaving 1 inch of headspace below the lid. It will be easier to pack the meat if you use wide-mouthed jars. Remember: Do not pack the meat tightly in the jar. If the meat is

packed too tightly, it may not cook thoroughly. Add salt at this time, unless you plan to salt the meat at the time that it is served. Consider using ½ teaspoon for pint jars and 1 teaspoon for quart jars.

6. Before placing lids on the jars, be sure the lips of the jars are clean and dry to facilitate the sealing process. Place lids on jars and screw on securing rings. There is no need to tighten excessively, as the ring is only being used to secure the lid until the vacuum in the jar seals the lid.

7. Place the jars in the pressure canner, ensuring that the jars do not touch each other. Fill the canner with water to the level prescribed by the instructions for your canner. Process the meat for the time and pressure prescribed for your elevation. Your pressure canner should have come with a time and pressure chart.

Time and Pressure Chart for Canning Wild Game

Pressure Canner with Dial Gauge

Pack Method	Jar Size	Time (min)	0 to 2,000 feet	2,001 to 4,000 feet	4,001 to 6,000 feet
Without bone Hot or raw	Pints	75	11 pounds	12 pounds	13 pounds
	Quarts	90	11 pounds	12 pounds	13 pounds
With bone Hot or raw	Pints	65	11 pounds	12 pounds	13 pounds
	Quarts	75	11 pounds	12 pounds	13 pounds

Pressure Canner with Weighted Gauge

Pack Method	Jar Size	Time	0 to 1,000 feet	above 1,000 feet
Without bone Hot or raw	Pints	75	10 pounds	15 pounds
	Quarts	90	10 pounds	15 pounds
With bone Hot or raw	Pints	75	10 pounds	15 pounds
	Quarts	90	10 pounds	15 pounds

CURING, DRYING, AND SMOKING BIG GAME ANIMALS

Procedures for curing and smoking meat from big game animals will be very similar to working with beef. There are special considerations when making homemade jerky from venison or other wild game, since venison can be heavily contaminated with fecal bacteria depending on the skill of the hunter in dressing the animal and the location of the wound. While fresh beef is usually rapidly chilled, deer carcasses are typically held at ambient temperatures, potentially allowing bacteria multiplication.

Recipes

Mom's Mostaccioli

This recipe was provided courtesy of Bill and Kay Tomaszewski. This recipe should feed eight to ten adults. If you cut the recipe in half, it should be sufficient for a family of four to six people. The commercially prepared canned items may be substituted with home-canned preserved items.

INGREDIENTS

10-ounce package of Mostaccioli noodles ....2 packages

15-ounce block chili
   (or the equivalent of your own chili) ....1 block

(Block chili is a solid chili mixture that is broken up and used in recipes like this, or liquefied and poured over rice, for example. Block chili may not be available in all areas, so you will need to substitute an equal amount of another chili product.)

Ground deer burger or ground beef.............................2 pounds

(You can make your deer burger with your own meat grinder after you begin cutting up your deer with your meat grinder, or you can have the facility that processes your deer meat make you sufficient ground deer burger for your uses.)

1-pound can of stewed tomatoes (drained) ....2 cans

10-ounce can tomato soup ....2 cans

Oregano ....1 teaspoon

Anise ....1 ½ teaspoons

Garlic ....2 cloves

Onions (chopped) ....2 large

Salt and pepper ....as needed

PREPARATION INSTRUCTIONS

1. Brown chopped onion and ground deer meat together in skillet. Then add oregano, anise, garlic, salt, and pepper. Cook until moisture disappears. It will take five to ten minutes to cook the meat.

2. Put chili, tomatoes, tomato soup, tomato sauce, and 1 ½ cups water together in pot. Cover and simmer slowly. Simmer for up to an hour so the spices have a chance to work.

3. Make Mostaccioli noodles. Drain and blanch with cold water. About fifteen minutes to cook noodles.

4. Mix all together and serve.

5. Garnish with parmesan cheese if desired.

Venison garlic sausage

This recipe was provided courtesy of North Dakota State University Extension and Julie Garden-Robinson.

INGREDIENTS

Pork trim 60/40 ....12 pounds

Venison trim ....10 pounds

Beef trim ....2 pounds

Water ....1 pint

Cure..1 ½ tablespoons

Salt...⅔ cups

Black Pepper ....4 tablespoons

Marjoram...2 teaspoons

Mustard Seed ....5 ½ teaspoons

Garlic..2 cloves or

½ teaspoon garlic powder

PREPARATION INSTRUCTIONS

1. Coarse-grind meat trimmings.

2. Add salt, water, cure, and spices to ground meat and mix thoroughly.

3. Regrind through ¼-inch diameter plate and stuff into pork casings.

4. Smoke product to desired color and heat to an internal temperature of 141 degrees Fahrenheit.

5. Store in refrigerator or freezer until use.

6. Product must be cooked before serving.

SAFETY PRECAUTIONS WHEN HARVESTING AND PRESERVING WILD GAME

The following list of diseases are some of the more common infections that can be contracted when handling wild game, or being out in the woods. The list may seem overpowering, but outdoors people who are knowledgeable and are willing to follow proper game handling procedures and good personal hygiene can reduce the risk to a very low level. The list is provided so that you can be well informed, and so that you will develop a greater desire to follow the safety rules when working with wild game.

Diseases associated with hunting and handling game

Anaplasmosis: Spread through tick bites. Well established in the western and eastern coasts especially. Symptoms similar to Lyme disease and include headaches, fever, chills, and muscles aches.

Avian Influenza: Humans who handle wild ducks are at risk for this disease. As of 2010, the risk seems to be low. Infection may not cause illness in healthy people. Other people may have flu-like symptoms.

Babesiosis: Transmitted by ticks and is hard to diagnose but causes flu-like symptoms. Found in Northeastern states and in Minnesota, Wisconsin, and Washington State.

Brucellosis: A disease found in bison, elk, reindeer, caribou, and other animals. Human brucellosis in the United States primarily comes from exposure to infected wild hogs and boars. Exposure comes during field cleaning of the animal. Protective gloves and eyewear should be used for personal protection.

Campylobacteriosis: A common foodborne infection that causes pain and cramps and can include bloody diarrhea. Found in raw milk, improperly cooked poultry, and water contaminated by fecal material.

Chronic wasting disease: *This disease was discussed in Chapter 1.*

Cryptosporidiosis: A disease caused by a one-cell parasite found in the stool of wild animals that are infected. Symptoms are extreme diarrhea, stomach cramps, nausea, vomiting, fever, headache, and decreased appetite.

Prevention is through good hygiene. Do not drink untreated water that infected animals have defecated in. Infected humans can transmit the disease in the same manner as animals. Never handle the infected fecal matter of either animals or humans without using protective gloves.

Deer parapoxvirus: Related viruses also affect sheep, goats, and cattle. Affected deer have scabby and crusty lesions on the muzzle, face, ears, neck, and antlers. Hunters have caught the disease when they nicked their hands with a knife during field cleaning. The hunters developed lesions on their hands.

E. coli: *This disease was discussed in Chapter 1.*

Giardiasis: Caused by microscopic parasites. Found in stools of domestic and wild animals. Infection in humans comes through contact with infected animal stool. Symptoms appear one to two weeks after infection and may last for two to six weeks. Symptoms are diarrhea, gas, stomach cramps, nausea, vomiting, and decreased appetite.

Lyme disease: Spread by bites from deer ticks. The earliest symptom is a rash that looks like a bull's-eye at the point of the bite. Symptoms include fever, headache, fatigue, and muscle and joint pain. The progression of the disease leads to chronic joint problems, heart problems, and neurological problems. People in the outdoors should protect themselves from tick bites.

Plague: This disease killed millions in the 1300s, and is still active in the environment. The disease is found in mountain lions, rodents, rabbits, and squirrels. Pneumonic plague is more serious than Bubonic plague, the former being a life threatening disease. Do not allow hunting dogs near prairie dog colonies to protect them from contracting this disease. The disease is spread by fleabites.

Q fever: The bacterium that causes this disease is found in sheep and goats. Birds and ticks also carry the disease. The nesting sites of infected animals provide a risk of transmission to humans. Infection in humans can come through drinking contaminated unpasteurized dairy products. Symptoms often are mistaken for a cold or flu and can involve the lungs, nervous system, and the heart.

Rocky Mountain spotted fever: Transmitted to people through tick bites. Symptoms appear three to 14 days after the bite of an infected tick. Symptoms are high fever, severe headache, fatigue, muscle aches, chills, and skin rash. Symptoms may last two to three weeks.

Salmonellosis (Salmonella): *This disease was discussed in Chapter 1.*

Toxoplasmosis: Caused by a single-cell parasite. Humans are infected by eating raw or undercooked venison, lamb, or pork. It can also be contracted through unpasteurized dairy products. Proper food handling procedures and proper personal hygiene are the best defense.

West Nile Virus: The virus starts in wild birds and is then transmitted to humans through tick and mosquito bites. Sudden bird die-offs are an indication the disease is present in an area. Hunters should avoid handling dead birds found in the wild that they have not shot.

CHAPTER 10:
Preserving Fish and Seafood

An important issue when considering the consumption of fish caught in some areas of the country is pollutants that can accumulate in the fatty areas of some fish. If a fish has accumulated pollutants, with proper preparation, such a fish can be safely consumed. People throughout the world consume large amounts of well-preserved fish and have developed many recipes. The goal of this chapter will be to bring to life many of these wonderful recipes.

Due to the similarities in seafood and fresh water fish preparation techniques, the two products have been combined into one chapter, although a good number of saltwater seafood varieties are greatly different than freshwater fish. This chapter will open many very interesting doors of discovery in the preparation and preservation of seafood.

There are many different kinds of fish and seafood that can be preserved.

HOW TO FREEZE FISH AND SEAFOOD

If you have access to freshly caught fish from ocean, lake, or stream, your food freezer can make it possible to have this delicious and nutritious food throughout most months of the year.

Fresh fish has firm, elastic flesh that resists indentation when pressed. The eyes are clear; gills are bright red; the skin is shiny. The scales adhere closely to the skin.

This fresh fish is being kept cool on ice.

How to prepare fish with scales for freezing

1. Beginning on the bottom side of the fish, at the rear just forward of the anal vent, make a slit forward toward the gills. Open the fish up and remove entrails, making sure that you scrape the backbone clean of all blood deposits. Put your thumb up inside the gills to hold the fish securely, and scrape off the scales using a fish scaler or the back of a heavy knife.

2. Remove gills, fins, head, and tail; wash fish thoroughly inside and out. Detailed instructions on cutting fillets are provided later in this chapter under the instructions for curing a fish.

3. Freeze whole steaks or fillets.

Brine dip for lean fish

Lean fish species are cod, sea bass, haddock, snapper, monkfish, hake, grouper, plaice, John Dory, whiting, sole, sea bream and most freshwater species. Lean fish species should be dipped in a brine solution before freezing to protect the firm texture of the meat and to reduce moisture loss in the freezer. A suggested brine solution is ¼ cup of salt per 2 quarts of water. The fish should only need to be dipped for no more than 30 seconds. This is a time measurement without any visual indication of how long you should keep the product in the brine solution.

Brine dip for fatty fish

Fish species that are considered high in fat content are salmon, tuna, halibut, mackerel, red mullet, herring, trout, eel, and sardines. These fish should be dipped in a brine solution of ascorbic acid before freezing to protect against rancidity caused by the high fat content. A suggested mixture of 2 tablespoons of ascorbic acid to 2 pints of water should be sufficient to complete this process. The same time measurement of 30 seconds applies to this process as with lean fish. This process is not designed to brine the fish for preservation but to firm up the meat for freezing. Fish must be refrigerated or exposed to a preservation process immediately after you get it home to ensure the product remains safe for your family to eat.

WHERE DO THE FISH COME FROM?

This is not meant to be an exhaustive list, but is merely a sample of some common fish you may be working with.

Cod: Found in the Atlantic Ocean along the East Coast.

Bass: Found in warm freshwater lakes throughout the United States.

Eel: Found in the Chesapeake Bay and East Coast rivers.

Haddock: Found in the Gulf of Maine.

Hake or whiting (Pacific whiting): Found in the Pacific Ocean off the West Coast.

Halibut: Found in the Pacific Northwest Coastal waters up to Alaska.

Herring: Found in coastal waters from Nova Scotia to Florida.

Grouper: Found in the waters off the coast of Florida.

John Dory: Found in the Chesapeake Bay to Nova Scotia.

Mackerel: Found in the Atlantic and Pacific oceans.

Monkfish: Found on the Atlantic Ocean floor.

Plaice: Found off the East Coast from Rhode Island to Maine.

Red Mullet: Found in the Mediterranean Sea and the northern Atlantic Ocean.

Salmon: Found on the East and West coasts and in large freshwater lakes throughout the United States.

Sardines: Found off the coast of Maine.

Sea Bass: Found in the ocean at 120 feet or deeper.

Sea Bream: Found from the Caribbean up through the Atlantic Coast.

Snapper: Found off the coast of Florida in the mangroves.

Sole: Found in the North Pacific coast area up to Alaska.

Trout: Found all across the United States in cool-water lakes and streams.

Tuna: Found in the Atlantic and Pacific oceans.

Methods of packaging fish

Fresh fish should be frozen the same day they are caught. To freeze, prepare the fish as you would for cooking; scale, clean, and wash it thoroughly. Behead and cut off the fins. Freeze small fish whole and cut large fish into steaks or fillets or leave whole for stuffing. Wrap in moisture/vapor-proof paper. Label the kind of fish, weight, and date. The flavor of fish is better if defrosted before cooking, although it can be cooked from the frozen state.

To make ice blocks, place several small fish, steaks, or fillets in a loaf pan or coffee tin and cover the fish with water before putting it in the freezer. When the blocks are frozen, remove the block from the pan and wrap the block in freezer packaging material to store. If you run warm water over the bottom of the pan, the fish block will easily drop out of the pan. Fish stored in this manner can stay in the freezer for three months before it should be thawed and consumed.

Ice glazing is another method commonly used to prepare fish for storage in the freezer. For a whole fish, freeze the fish unwrapped. Dip frozen fish in chilled water, just above the freezing point. Repeat the dipping until a glaze of ⅛- to ¼-inch thick ice has formed. Wrap in moisture/vapor-proof material or seal in plastic bag. Fish may be packaged (in meal-sized portions) with any moisture/vapor-proof material. Moisture/vapor-proof freezer packaging includes: aluminum foil, polyethylene bags, freezer film wraps, plastic, and metal containers. Ice glazing does not protect the product in the freezer as well as an ice block will. The thin ice glaze can be chipped off, increasing the chance of the product getting freezer burn. You will need to either keep the ice glaze from being chipped off or put the fish in a container that will protect the glaze. The fish in an ice glaze will remain stable in the freezer as long as the glaze is not chipped off. Ice-glazed products that have been exposed should be thawed and cooked as soon as possible.

If lobsters are prepared for freezing properly, they can be kept in the freezer for up to 12 months. When preparing to freeze lobsters, you should always begin with lobsters that are alive and chilled. The lobster must be blanched in water that has been heated to 212 degrees for at least 60 seconds. The blanching solution is 2 percent salt brine (with non-iodized salt). After the lobster has been blanched, it is to be chilled using running water, or you can use a 50/50 mix of water and ice in a tub large enough to immerse the lobster. Then you place the lobster in a freezer bag and remove as much air as possible to prevent freezer burn. When you get ready to cook the lobster, you should allow the lobster to thaw in the refrigerator. After the lobster has thawed completely, boil it in 2 percent salt brine for 12 to 15 minutes.

Fresh shrimp may be frozen cooked or uncooked, with or without their shell. Whether you freeze your shrimp cooked or uncooked is a matter of preference, not of the quality of the product. The head and large dark vein must be removed as soon as possible to protect the meat from contamination. For longer storage, it is best to pour water over the package of frozen shrimp and thaw them just enough to pull them out of the package. At this point, pour water over the shrimp to glaze them, return them to the package, and put them back in the freezer. Pack in freezer cartons or bags. Label weight and date.

These frozen shrimp will make a tasty addition to a shrimp scampi dish.

The following are instructions for shelling and deveining fresh shrimp:

1. Start by pulling off the shrimp's head using your thumb and forefinger.

2. Pull off the legs.

3. Begin at the head end of the shrimp and pull the outer shell off. Some people will leave the last segment of the shell and tail on for decorative purposes.

4. The shell can be left on by using a pair of scissors and cutting along the outer edge of the shrimp's back. You will cut the shell sufficiently to remove the dark vein. Some people prefer the flavor of the shrimp with the shell on during cooking.

5. Use a small, sharp paring knife to cut along the outer edge of the shrimp's back ¼ inch deep.

6. If you are able to see the dark vein, with the aid of your paring knife, pull the dark vein out and throw it away. It is located under the surface of the back. If there is no vein present, it is okay. Return the shelled and deveined shrimp to your bowl of ice or water and work on the next one.

When freezing raw shrimp in their shells, wash and remove the head and large veins. Then wash again in a saltwater solution of 2 tablespoons to 1 quart of cold water. Drain thoroughly and package, label, and freeze.

When freezing cooked shrimp, you should wash it in salted water after the head and veins have been removed. The shrimp is put in the brine solution to preserve a firm texture of the meat. A typical brine solution is ¼ cup of salt to 2 pints of water. Do not leave the shrimp in the brine solution for more than 20 minutes. Then drain and cook the shrimp in boiling water for ten minutes. After the shrimp have cooled down, remove the shell and the dark veins if they were not removed previously. Rinse again and allow the shrimp to cool before freezing. A point to remember is that cooked shrimp that has been stored in the freezer may toughen slightly.

Oysters, clams, and scallops should be frozen only if very fresh. Discard shells, and do not wash clams or oysters. Scallops may be rinsed in fresh water. Pack in freezer cartons or bags. Label weight and date.

How to freeze crabs

The key to successfully preparing and freezing crabs is to remember that crabmeat is very perishable. Speed is the key to success once you start the process. Leaving crabmeat out on the counter for even a short time will allow dangerous bacteria to grow in the meat. If you plan to freeze whole crabs, it will be necessary to clean the crab before boiling or blanching. Boil live crabs for about 20 minutes in saltwater. Crabs can be cooked whole or in pieces. Crabmeat should not be kept in the freezer for more than three months; otherwise, the product begins to lose its flavor and wholesomeness. When the crab is placed in the freezer bag, leave a little air in the bag for expansion of the product.

IMPORTANT STEPS TO CONSIDER WHEN CANNING SEAFOOD AND FRESHWATER FISH

- One to 3 tablespoons of vegetable oil or a French dressing can be added to each pint jar to enhance the flavor of the meat.

- Fish and seafood must be canned in pint and half-pint jars since safe processing times have not been established for quart jars.

- After you have put the jars in the pressure canner, exhaust the air in the canner by allowing a stream of steam to flow from the petcock for at least ten minutes. Processing time does not begin until this venting is complete.

- After the meat has been processed the correct length of time, let the pressure return to zero before attempting to open the lid.

- Make sure the pressure remains constant during the entire processing time. Weighted gauges should jiggle or rock indicating constant pressure.

Pressure Canner Chart for Seafood and Freshwater Fish

Processing Time	½ Pint Jar	Pint Jar	Pressure Adjustment for Weighted Gauge Canner
Raw fish	100 min.	100 min.	**0 to 1,000 feet:** 10 pounds
Whole clams	60 min.	70 min.	**Above 1,000 feet:** 15 pounds

Processing Time	½ Pint Jar	Pint Jar	Pressure Adjustment for Dial Gauge Canner
Minced clams	60 min.	70 min.	**0 to 2,000 feet: 11 pounds**
Crab	70 min.	80 min.	**2,001 to 4,000 feet: 12 pounds**
Oysters	75 min.	75 min.	**4,001 to 6,000 feet: 13 pounds**
Shrimp	45 min.	45 min.	**6,001 to 8,000 feet: 14 pounds**

Recipes

Fish stock

*This recipe was provided courtesy of David G. Blackburn of **www.canningusa.com**.*

This fish stock is a convenient product to have at home to make paella or fish soup. Paella is a dish that originates from a region in Spain. With seafood, it is a mixture of white rice, green vegetables, beans, and seasonings. This product should not be made with oily fish such as tuna, salmon, mackerel, trout, or bluefish.

INGREDIENTS

	PINT	QUART
Fish including bones, head and tail	1 pound	2 pounds
Onion, medium diced	½	1
Carrot, medium diced	½	1
Celery stalk, diced	¼	1
Parsley, finely chopped	2 tablespoons	¼ cup
Salt	¼ teaspoon	½ teaspoon
Dry white cooking wine	¼ cup	½ cup
Water	1 ¼ cup	1 ¼ quart
Lemon Juice	1 tablespoon	2 tablespoons
Bay leaves	½	1

PREPARATION INSTRUCTIONS

1. Start by using a large pot; add all the ingredients and bring to a simmer.

2. Simmer for one hour, skimming and discarding any residue at the top of the mixture.

3. Skim and strain the mixture through cheesecloth, and then can using the hot-pack method with 1 inch of headspace.

4. Process with a pressure canner for 30 minutes for pints, or 35 minutes for quarts, at 11 pounds of pressure.

5. For elevations above 1,000 feet, use the pressure and altitude adjustments chart in Chapter 2.

Canned salmon

*This recipe was provided courtesy of David G. Blackburn of **www.canningusa.com**.*

SPECIAL INSTRUCTIONS

Make sure the salmon you use is fresh and has been kept on ice until you are ready to begin the canning process. This recipe would also work for other fatty fish.

INGREDIENTS

SIZE OF JAR	½ PINT	PINT
Salmon (approximate weight per canning jar)	10 ounce	20 ounce
Salt	½ teaspoon	1 teaspoon

PREPARATION INSTRUCTIONS

1. Fillet, debone, and wash fish. You may discard the skin if you like.

2. Cut fish into three to four pieces and salt as desired.

3. Raw pack in jars, leaving 1 inch of headspace. Fill up to 1 inch of headspace with water or oil.

4. Process with a pressure canner for 100 minutes at 11 pounds of pressure, or 10 pounds for a weighted gauge.

5. *See the altitude and pressure adjustment chart provided earlier in this chapter for elevations over 1,000 feet.*

CURING, DRYING, AND SMOKING FISH AND SEAFOOD

The process of curing meat is one that began many centuries ago but has dramatically changed over the years. The basic definition of curing, as it pertains to preparing meat or fish, is the application of salt and other seasonings, as well as color-fixing ingredients, in order to get a distinct smell and flavor as a result.

Mankind has a long history of preserving meat through curing and smoking. People in the past hung salted meat and fish over a campfire to preserve their meat for use at a later time. Modern man still uses some of the same techniques but has now added nitrates and other preservative agents that modern science has provided. Smoking and drying techniques and equipment have been greatly improved also. The idea is the same: to preserve good tasting and nutritious food for use at a later date.

For centuries, one of the most reliable food sources has been smoke-cured fish. People were able to develop curing and smoking techniques long before the advent of refrigeration. They were able to catch fish when they were abundant and preserve them by smoke-curing for use when other food sources were unavailable. Through the use of smoke-cured fish, people were able to stay alive.

This dried cod looks intimidating, but has a nice, full flavor.

Recipes

How to prepare smoked fish

GENERAL INSTRUCTIONS

Earlier in this chapter, a list of saltwater and freshwater fish was provided. Any fish species on the list can be cured and smoked. Salmon and trout are good for smoking because of their high fat content. These fish will absorb smoke much better than some of the others. Salmon has been a favorite for smoking for centuries. For your family's safety, you are encouraged to follow all of the sanitation procedures that were discussed throughout the book. *In Chapter 1, you will find detailed sanitation rules for the kitchen.* All of your cooking utensils, cooking pans, and kitchen counters need to be clean and sanitary. Make sure that your fish remains refrigerated except during the times you are actually involved in processing your fish to inhibit the growth of microorganisms and dangerous bacteria. As soon as the actual curing and smoking process is begun, the smoke and heat will prevent bacteria from growing, so refrigeration is not a concern until you remove your fish from the smoker. The next step is to prepare your fish for curing. Earlier in this chapter, a step-by-step description of how to clean a fish was provided. After you finish cleaning your fish, you will need to decide if the fish will be smoked whole, or if you will need to cut fillets from the fish.

Here are step-by-step instructions for filleting a fish:

- Place the fish on a cutting board large enough to hold the entire fish. Fillet boards can be purchased at sporting goods stores; they have clips to slip the head of the fish under to aid in holding the fish still while you cut the fillet.

- Use a thin, flexible, sharp kitchen knife or a fillet knife to make the actual cut down the body of the fish. The cutting motion will be from the head of the fish toward the tail.

- Begin the cut at the back of the head using a slight sawing motion and slide the knife along the backbone without cutting into any of the rib bones. You will need to proceed slowly at first. The goal is to remove the meat from the rib cage without picking up any bones. Do not include the tail in the fillet.

- Carefully pick the fillet up behind the head and gently pull it away from the fish as you use the knife to make small cuts that will release any place where the fillet is sticking to the bones. Again, you want as much meat as possible without getting bones in the fillet.

- Repeat these steps on the opposite side of the fish.

- If you do not want the skin left on your fillet, with the aid of the knife, carefully separate the skin from both of the fillets. The skin should separate from the meat without too much trouble if you pull gently and use the knife to cut free any areas that are sticking together. Use the knife, your fingers, and maybe a pair of tweezers you have sanitized to check for any bones you may have in the fillet.

- You may need to practice on several fish before you become an expert at filleting fish.

Fish are cured the same way you would cure any other meat. The difference is that you will be working with much smaller pieces of meat. Throughout the book, several curing formulas have been described. Your fish fillets can be dry-salted or put in a brine solution, but the differences in the size of your fish fillet will determine the intensity of the salt cure you will use. The length of time your fillets are exposed to the wet or dry cure will also determine how much salt is absorbed into the meat. The following instructions for dry curing fish instruct you to keep the fish in the cure for 24 hours. If you only want a light salt cure, you may decide to leave the fish in the salt for 12 hours. If you want a heavy cure to soak into the fish, you may decide to leave it in the dry cure a few hours longer.

This is a lot of information to digest, so a good suggestion is to find a professionally developed cure for your fish. A prepackaged fish cure formula will provide you with explicit directions on how to use the product.

This salted cod is ready for sale at the market.

Dry cure compound for whole fish

This recipe and procedure is the creation of the author.

INGREDIENTS

Salt...2 pounds

Sugar..¾ pound (You can experiment
with the sugar concentration)

Saltpeter...½ ounce

Sodium nitrate ....¼ ounce

Note: For smaller quantities of fish, simply halve the formulation. *A weight and measurement conversion chart is provided at the end of Chapter 2.*

PREPARATION INSTRUCTIONS

1. Thoroughly mix all of the dry cure ingredients together.

2. Use a deep plastic tub or a stoneware dish that will not react with the salt for your curing container.

3. Place a plastic shelf in the bottom of the container that has vent holes so the brine can drain away from the fish. Support the shelf so it has about 1 inch of clearance from the bottom of the container.

4. Rub the dry cure mixture over all surfaces of the fillets, or over the whole fish, and place in the curing container. You will need to use a cure injector to get cure deep inside the fish if you are trying to achieve a heavily cured product. If you will have sufficient fish to need to layer the fish, cover each layer generously with the dry cure mixture.

5. Cover the dish or plastic tub and place in the refrigerator for up to 24 hours. The curing process will develop liquid brine at the bottom of the pan.

6. When you take the fish out of the dry cure, lightly rinse the salt off and set the fish out on a clean counter on paper towels to air-dry.

Brine cure procedures

INGREDIENTS

Cold water ....3 gallons

Salt...2 pounds

Sugar...¾ cup

Saltpeter ....½ ounce

Sodium nitrate ....¼ ounce

PREPARATION INSTRUCTIONS

1. Thoroughly mix the ingredients. Ensure the salt and sugar is completely dissolved. Add more water if the salt and sugar are not completely dissolving. You can do a little experimentation over time to find the exact mixture that works best for you. Also, different types of salt will dissolve at different ratios.

2. Consider how much brine you need to make to cover the amount of fish you have to cure.

3. Use a plastic tub or crock that will not react to the salt. Pour about 1 inch of brine into the bottom of the container.

4. Place the fish into the container layer by layer, and pour the rest of the brine into the container. You may need to weigh the fish down to ensure that it remains covered completely by the brine mixture. Do not pack the fish into the brine container too tightly. The brine needs to be able to soak through to all parts of the fish.

5. Place the brining fish in a refrigerator for the complete brining process. For safety's sake, the fish must stay below 40 degrees Fahrenheit. If the refrigerator does not have a large enough space for the brine pan, find a large enough container to hold the brining container and pack ice around the brining container.

6. If you use a pre-packaged fish cure, the instructions will tell you how long to leave the fish under the influence of the curing process. If you use a homemade curing formula, then you will need to determine how long to leave the fish in the cure. For example, a ¼-pound fillet should be fully cured in 30 minutes, 2 pounds of fish in three hours, and 5 pounds of fish in eight hours.

7. After you have cured the fish, rinse it off with clean, cold water and allow it to dry. After the fish dries, a pellicle or glazed appearance will tell you the fish is ready for the smoker. Use a small fan to reduce

the drying time. Remember, the fish are not in a refrigerator during the drying time. The fish are fully cured at this point, but you must always err on the side of caution. If your smoker has racks for the fish to lie on, then use the smoker to dry the fish.

8.   If there will be a long delay before you begin smoking the fish, it will be necessary to place the fish in the refrigerator. If you had salted the fish sufficiently to not require refrigeration, the level of salt in the meat would adversely affect the taste.

Cold smoking

The temperature inside the smoker should be brought to 80 degrees Fahrenheit, but under no circumstances should you allow the temperature to rise above 90 degrees. The fish should be left in the smoker until all the pieces have the same brown color. Smaller fish portions may reach this stage in 24 hours, whereas larger pieces may take up to four days of continual smoking to be finished. If you have used your smoker many times, you will have a feeling for how to proceed. If you are an inexperienced smoker, remember that during the first 12 hours you should keep the level of smoke low. After the first 12 hours, you should increase the production of smoke. When increasing the smoke, do not increase the heat. When the fish is finished, the finished product should be safe to store under refrigeration for several weeks. Please remember, cold smoking is not cooking, so the fish will still need to be cooked before you eat it.

Hot smoking

Start by heating your smoker to about 90 degrees. If you have a commercial smoker, follow the directions that came with the smoker. Place the fish on the shelves in the smoker and leave in the 90-degree heat for about two hours. At this point, the fish should have taken on a brown color similar to what happens during cold smoking. Gradually bring the temperature in the smoker up to 175 degrees. There are two indications that your fish are done: when the internal temperature of the fish reaches 140 degrees, and when the meat will flake off when you press it with a knife or fork. Small pieces of fish may be done in as little as four hours, while large pieces or whole fish may take up to eight hours. When the smoking process is complete, remove the fish and set it somewhere to cool off before you put it in the refrigerator. Since hot-smoked fish is fully cooked, you will not need to cook it again before serving. Although it is cooked, you will probably want to heat it up before you eat it. Your smoked fish product will keep in the refrigerator several days before you consume it, and it will keep in the freezer for several months.

These salted herrings were caught in coastal waters.

SAFETY PRECAUTIONS WHEN PRESERVING FISH AND SEAFOOD

Safe handling of fish begins when it is caught. When you are landing a fish, avoid harsh bumping of fish against rocks, boat sides, or dock structures to prevent bruising. Fish that are badly bruised lose their texture and have increased risk of spoilage in the areas that are bruised. As soon as possible, rinse and clean the fish in fresh, clean water. Avoid using water from around docks or municipal drains that is dirty or has an oily appearance. After the fish is cleaned, chill promptly and put under ice or refrigeration as soon as possible to inhibit the growth of bacteria.

Fish store pollutants absorbed from polluted water in the fatty deposits in their body. State fishing pamphlets usually provide information and warnings about fisheries that contain unsafe contaminants and tips on how to protect yourself and your family. Because of contaminant levels in state fisheries; there are specific advisories about how much of different species of fish women of child-bearing age and nursing mothers should eat, for example. If your state does not provide warnings such as this, then you are free to consume the fish you catch without any problems. Even in areas with consumption advisories, if you follow the stated precautions, you can still catch some fish for the enjoyment of your family.

Conclusion

When this project began, it was impossible to know exactly what the finished product would look like. The original plan or thought was to include basic and advanced information on the art of preparing and preserving a wide range of meats, and to provide as many recipes as possible. As the book developed, it became a far more technical presentation of the art of meat preservation than was envisioned. As it turned out, the technical aspect of the book should provide people with a complete source for all aspects of preserving nourishing and wholesome food for their family.

The technical issues are very important when a discussion of food preparation is taking place. Everybody wants to enjoy the great bounty of meat available in the United States without having to worry if the food is going to make a person seriously ill. Food safety standards and home meat preserving procedures are constantly being updated to ensure everyone can harvest, prepare, and preserve completely safe and wholesome foods for their family's enjoyment.

The place to start thinking about food safety is when the meat is picked up at the store, or when you are cleaning the game or fish that you just caught. Meat picked up from the store should not be allowed to sit for a long time in your car before it is put back in the refrigerator or freezer at home. Freshly harvested game and fish need to be cleaned and put under refrigeration as soon as possible. Many people like to hang a deer in the garage for a few days before taking it to the meat plant or taking it in the house to cut up and process. Be cautious about leaving a carcass hanging in the garage for several days if the weather turns warm. You do not want the meat you worked so hard to get to become spoiled.

Every kitchen utensil, countertop, or pan that will be used needs to be cleaned and sanitized before using them to process your meat. Be aware of cross-contamination of different food products that may be on the countertop. Juice from uncooked poultry that is sitting on the countertop can be easily transferred to a piece of beef if you are not careful. Remember to wash your hands often and before you move from one project to another.

When you are cooking or smoking meats, always remember the rule about the internal temperature of what you are cooking. Just because it looks done on the outside does not mean that it is cooked thoroughly enough to serve and eat. Meat products that reach the proper internal cooking temperature have reached a point where you can say with confidence that they are free from harmful bacteria that could have made you and your family very ill.

A few words about recipes are in order also. Every recipe in this book came from somebody's idea for something good to eat. None of the recipe ideas are original to this author. When you see a recipe in the book that is accredited to someone, think about going to that person's Web site and saying thank you for allowing us to share that recipe with the world. Also remember that you can always tweak a recipe a little bit to bring out a flavor that you personally enjoy. Just keep in mind the basic premise that food safety rules cannot be avoided.

Beyond all of the technical information, one of the goals of this book was to enhance the importance of the family by providing encouragement for people to preserve meat according to time-honored traditions. The few family memories that were shared in the preface of the book are the kind of memories that build solid family relationships. Even after all of these years, my children will bring those events up when we are sitting around the table talking about "the good old days." By involving your children in the process, you can give your family similar memories.

The rush of American society to embrace rapid technological advancements is in some ways dehumanizing the human experience. Only the people who lived prior to World War II will remember the types of food preparation experiences like the ones recounted in the case studies from Eugene Oster and Helen Pyell Ibsen. In those days, everybody knew that all types of food come from the land. If you ask a young person today where food comes from, they will often answer, "The grocery store." Americans are rapidly being removed from direct contact with the land, which is the source of all the food that nourishes our nation. Reinvigorating an interest in harvesting and preserving meat is a great way to bring your family's focus back on things that make us human.

Another goal of this book was to present meat preservation techniques as a wonderful art form. Everyone likes good food, and everyone has deep respect for the person who is a good cook, and of course nobody is interested in eating food prepared by someone who is a terrible cook. The basics of cooking can be mastered with a little practice. By the same token, the basic meat preservation techniques presented in this book can be mastered with some effort. In the fish section, there are basic instructions for filleting a fish. It may take several fish before you become qualified at filleting fish, but keep trying, and do not give up.

A person who has a successful season of harvesting and putting up the meat in canning jars, or in the freezer, or has many packages of cured or smoked meat, can justifiably look upon the fruits of his or her labors with pride. Can you remember your grandmother's shelves filled with all kinds of canned foods she had spent the chilly fall days preparing? That is truly a beautiful picture to behold. Then think about the days when you got to see some of those jars opened and wonderfully good food was poured out into the pan on the kitchen stove to heat up and be prepared to eat. The true testimony of the love and art that goes into preserving good food comes in the cold, dark days of winter when you reach up on the shelf and take down a jar of beef that has been canned and make that very special beef stew that not only warms and fills the body, but also instills a deep warmth into your and your family's hearts.

If this book has been successful in accomplishing the things that were discussed here, then the entire project can be considered a success. For you who are experienced and qualified at the art of meat preservation, please find someone you can share your skill with and keep these important traditions alive for future generations. For the beginner, just pick out a project that you think you can safely start with and start cooking and preparing wonderful meat items for the enjoyment of your family and friends.

APPENDIX:
Resources

FOOD PRESERVATION INFORMATION

Beef Culinary Center: The Cattlemen's Beef Board and National Cattlemen's Beef Association. This source will provide a description of the different types of veal that are on the market in the United States. *www.beefandvealculinary.com/vealtypes.aspx*

The National Center for Home Food Preservation: Freezing Meats. This is a very good resource for information on how to freeze meat and fish properly. *www.uga.edu/nchfp/how/freeze/meat.html*

The National Center for Home Food Preservation: Smoking and Curing, the University of Georgia. This is a very practical resource for information on the science of food preservation. Home preservers need to understand the how to prepare nutritious and safe food for their family. *www.uga.edu/nchfp/publications/nchfp/lit_rev/cure_smoke_cure.html*

University of Illinois Extension: Meat Temperature Chart. This is a useful chart to help you cook your meat to a safe internal temperature. If you explore around this site, you will find a wealth of information on cooking. *http://web.extension.illinois.edu/meatsafety/preparation/tempchart.html*

University of Illinois Meat Science and Muscle Biology. This is a very technical resource for information on the science of meat. This is a great resource for the person who needs to understand the fine details of food preservation science. *http://labs.ansci.illinois.edu/meatscience*

University of Minnesota Extension. This site provides a wealth of information on preparing food safely. *www.extension.umn.edu/FoodSafetyEd*

United States Department of Agriculture: Food Safety and Inspection Service. This site contains very important information on the safety issues on cooking food. *www.fsis.usda.gov/factsheets*

FOOD PRESERVATION EQUIPMENT

All American Pressure Canner. A resource to purchase a quality pressure canner. A pressure canner is essential for canning meats. *www.allamericancanner.com/allamericanpressurecanner.htm*

Ball Canning Jars. This is the place to go for your entire jar and lid supply needs. This site will display all the canning jars that are currently being manufactured. *www.freshpreserving.com*

BBQ Trader. This is a great place to find all the barbecue equipment you will ever need. There are many wonderful things in this resource for the home meat preserver to discover. *www.bbqtrader.com*

Bernardin. This is the place for everybody in Canada to look for canning supplies. Bernardin is a member of the Ball Canning Jar family. *www.bernadin.ca*

Cabela's. This is a place to find a wide range of products you will need to hunt, preserve food, and any other outdoor items you may need. *www.cabelas.com/catalog/browse/home-cabin/_/N-1101235*

Cutlery and More. This company is a source for high-quality Zwilling J. A. Henckels knives. *www.cutleryandmore.com/henckels.htm*

Gunter Wilhelm Cutlery. This is another source for high-quality knives. *http://gunterwilhelm.com/Shop-Cutlery/cutlery_listItems.asp? idCategory=Cutlery+Sets*

Presto Pressure Canner. A good place to begin looking for a high-quality pressure canner; this site has a wide range of products to choose from. *www.pressurecooker-outlet.com/prestopressurecanner.htm*

MetroKitchen. This company is a place to purchase quality Wusthof knives. If you are going to work with meat and fish, you will need a quality set of knives. *www.metrokitchen.com/wusthof*

Thunderbird Meat Grinders. Anyone who is going to get into the art of sausage making will need a good quality meat grinder; this is a great place to find exactly the meat grinder you need. *www.yourdelight.com/ thunderbird_meat_grinders.htm*

Tupperware: Freezer Containers and Cold Food Storage. For everyone who enjoys using Tupperware, this is a good place to look for just the container you need to put some meat in the freezer. *http://order.tupperware.com/coe-html/webdex/freezer.html*

U.S. Plastic Corp: Stor-Keeper Containers with Lids. This is another great resource for all the plastic containers that can be used in the kitchen for food preservation projects. *www.usplastic.com*

FOOD PRESERVATION SUPPLIES

Allied Kenco Sales. This company has a wide variety of products that are designed to help you prepare and preserve meat. *www.alliedkenco.com/ catalog/index.php*

Butcher and Packer Supply Company. This is another good source of meat preservation products and supplies. *www.butcher-packer.com*

Food Saver Vacuum Sealing System. This is another product that can help you prepare your meat product for the freezer. The person who is serious about freezing meat and fish will need the best possible quality freezer preservation supplies. *www.foodsaver.com/Index.aspx*

Freezer Bags. This company is a great supplier for freezer bags. The safest way to preserve your meat and fish is with quality freezer bags. *www.shopwiki.com/Freezer+Bags*

The Sausage Maker Inc. This company can help you get a good start as a sausage maker or help old pros find the supplies they need. *www.sausagemaker.com*

The TNT Dakotah Sausage Stuffer. This is a company that will provide you with recipes and instructions on sausage making, along with a place to find some important equipment you will need. *www.dakotahsausagestuffer.com/smksaus.htm*

Wenneman Meat Company. This is a good place for supplies in Illinois and for everyone who has access to the Internet. Take some time and explore their Web site and look at all of the quality meats and preservation supplies they have for sale. *www.wenneman.com*

BIG GAME HUNTING INFORMATION FROM ALL ACROSS NORTH AMERICA

Alaskan brown bear: Contact the Alaska Division of Wildlife Conservation for hunting information. *www.wildlife.alaska.gov/index.cfm?adfg=bears.main*

Alaska/Yukon moose: Contact the Alaska Division of Wildlife Conservation for hunting information. *www.wildlife.alaska.gov/index.cfm?adfg=moosehunting.main*

American alligator: The Georgia Department of Natural Resources Wildlife Resources Division Web site provides specific field dressing instructions to remove the parts of the animal where mercury would be deposited. *www.georgiawildlife.com/node/610*

Barren ground caribou: Contact the Alaska Division of Wildlife Conservation for hunting information. *www.wildlife.alaska.gov/index.cfm?adfg=caribou.main*

Black bear: Contact the Minnesota Department of Natural Resources for hunting information. *www.dnr.state.mn.us/hunting/bear/index.html*

Blacktail deer: Contact the Alaska Division of Wildlife Conservation for hunting information. *www.wildlifenews.alaska.gov/index.cfm?adfg=wildlife_news.view_article&issue_id=22&articles_id=109*

Bighorn sheep: Contact the Arizona Game and Fish Department for hunting information. *www.azgfd.gov/w_c/bhsheep/hunting.shtml*

Bison: Contact the Montana Fish, Wildlife, and Parks Department for hunting information. *http://fwp.mt.gov/hunting/hunt.html*

Canada moose: Contact Canada North Lodge for hunting information. *www.canada-north.com/moose.htm*

Coues deer: Contact the Arizona Game and Fish Department for hunting information. *www.azgfd.gov/h_f/game_cues.shtml*

Cougar: Contact the Washington State Department of Fish and Wildlife for hunting information. *http://wdfw.wa.gov/hunting/bear_cougar/index.html*

Dall's sheep: Contact the Alaska Department of Fish and Game for hunting information. *www.adfg.state.ak.us/pubs/notebook/biggame/dallshee.php*

Desert bighorn sheep: Contact the Big Game Outfitters in Mexico for hunting information. *www.huntmexico.com*

Grizzly bear: Contact the Alaska Division of Wildlife Conservation for hunting information. *www.wc.adfg.state.ak.us/index.cfm?adfg=blackbear.blackbrown*

Mountain caribou: Contact the Indian River Ranch Guides and Outfitters in Canada for hunting information. *www.irrhunting.com/mountain_caribou_hunts.htm*

Mountain goat: Contact the Idaho Fish and Game Department for hunting information. *http://fishandgame.idaho.gov/ifwis/huntplanner/biggame.aspx?ID=8*

Mule deer: Contact the Colorado Division of Wildlife for hunting information. *http://wildlife.state.co.us/WildlifeSpecies/Profiles/Mammals/Deer.htm*

Musk ox: Contact the High Arctic Lodge for hunting information. *www.higharctic.com/hunting.htm*

Pronghorn antelope: Contact Wyoming Trophy Hunts for hunting information. *www.wy-trophyhunts.com*

Rocky Mountain elk: Contact the U.S. National Forest Service at Ashley National Forest for hunting information. *www.fs.fed.us/r4/ashley/recreation/flaming_gorge/fg_web_pages/Hunting/hunting.shtml*

Roosevelt's elk: Contact Hunt Washington State.com for hunting information. *www.huntwashingtonstate.com/HWS/big%20Game/Roosevelt%20Elk%20Tips.htm*

Tule elk: Contact the California Department of Fish and Game for hunting information. *www.dfg.ca.gov/wildlife/hunting/elk/tule*

Whitetail deer: Contact the New Hampshire Fish and Game Department for hunting information. *www.wildlife.state.nh.us/Hunting/Hunt_species/hunt_deer.htm*

Glossary of Meat Preservation and Cooking Terms

Aging: A process used to improve the quality of a meat product by allowing it to hang at ambient temperature for a short period of time. People expect an enhancement of flavor through this process.

Aluminum silicate: A mineral salt that is used to keep dried milk in vending machines from caking. Although consumption of small amounts of this additive has not been found to present a serious health risk, reproductive and development problems have been found in experimental animals exposed to aluminum compounds.

Amino acids: These compounds are used to fortify processed vegetables and are important to the human body in the correct combinations.

Ammonium carbonates: Used in baked goods, in confectionary items, and in ice cream. These chemicals can affect the mucous membrane and can contribute to the loss of calcium and magnesium from the human body.

Alkaline phosphate: Used to increase the pH factor in meat and increase the amount of water meat products will hold.

Anaplasmosis: A disease spread to humans through tick bites. Symptoms are similar to Lyme disease. This disease is well established in the upper Midwest and Northeastern United States.

Antimicrobials: Used to prevent the growth of molds and bacteria.

Antioxidants: Used to keep foods from turning rancid and developing dark spots, and to aid in preventing the loss of important vitamins. Proponents of antioxidants claim significant health benefits from consuming these agents.

Avian influenza: Humans who handle infected waterfowl are at risk of contracting this disease. Although the present risk is low, people who are infected will experience flu-like symptoms.

Babesiosis: This disease is transmitted by ticks and is difficult to diagnose because its symptoms are so closely related to symptoms of the flu. Found in the Northeastern states, upper Midwest, and Washington state.

Bacteria: Not visible to the human eye unaided, they are the primary agents in the biological process on the planet that break down and recycle nutrients.

Biological process: This is the natural process of all the biological elements in a meat product breaking the meat down to smaller elements. This process is facilitated by improper storage and preservation methods.

Blooming: Sausage is hung on sticks in a cool place for seven to ten days to reach the desired texture and color.

Boudin: There are a number of sausages that come under this title. These products are made of pork and may or may not use the blood of the animal.

Bratwurst: Pork-based German sausage seasoned for a specific taste.

Browning meat: The process of searing the surface of meat, chicken, or fish to seal in moisture and to prepare the meat for cooking in a pressure canner or to roast in the oven.

Brucellosis: Disease found in bison, elk, reindeer, and caribou. Most human exposure in the United States is through exposure to infected wild hogs. Exposure also comes during field dressing of an animal carcass.

Butcher: This is a person who cuts meat from a slaughtered animal carcass and prepares the cuts for retail sale.

Butylated hydroxyanisole (BHA) and butylated hydroxytoluene (BHT): Used to inhibit fats and oils in foods from becoming rancid.

Calicvirus or Norwalk-like viruses: Cause a very common form of foodborne illness called gastroenteritis. This disease is rarely diagnosed because most labs do not have the necessary tests available. This disease causes acute gastrointestinal illness with vomiting and diarrhea. The disease is usually over in two days for most people. This disease is passed from person to person through kitchen workers handling food products with unwashed hands.

Campylobacter: This is found in the intestines of healthy birds. This bacterial pathogen is almost always found in uncooked poultry of any variety. The symptoms of the illness it causes will include fever, diarrhea, and abdominal cramps. Humans contract this disease by eating raw or undercooked chicken and other poultry. Additionally, other foods are infected when they come in contact with juices dripping from affected uncooked chicken and poultry. When handling raw poultry, it is essential to contain drippings from the bird and sanitize any kitchen surfaces uncooked poultry juices have dripped on.

Campylobacteriosis: One of the most common bacterial infections that humans are affected by. The disease comes from consumption of infected food. Can come from undercooked poultry or contact with animal feces. It may be serious enough to cause bloody diarrhea.

Canning: A process designed to safely cook and seal food in airtight jars for storage for use at a later date.

Canning jars: Glass jars designed to secure and seal, safely keeping foods preserved for a family's use many months after the meat or produce was harvested.

Canning pressure cooker: A large pressure cooker that allows the home preserver to fill canning jars with various meats to raise the product to high enough temperature to sanitize the canning jars and at the same time cook the meat fully.

Capicola: An Italian cold cut made from the shoulder or neck meat.

Chemical process: In meat preservation, this is the change that takes place in the molecular structure that is produced by the application of preservation techniques and processes.

Chevon: This is the Spanish and official word for goat meat.

Cold smoking: Adding flavor and preserving meat with wood smoke without sufficient heat to cook the meat.

Collagen: Used to make sausage casings. Made from fibers derived from different animal by-products including bone, tendons, and intestinal tract organs.

Contamination: This describes the condition when the meat being preserved has been in contact with dirt or some disease-causing organism or chemical.

Curing: This is the process of preserving meat and fish by the application of salt, nitrates, sugar, or other commercially applied chemical additives.

Chorizo: A sausage of Spanish origin that may or may not be cooked; some people use it to replace ground beef or pork.

Chronic Wasting Disease: A neurological disease that infects deer and elk populations. It can cause behavioral problems and even death. This disease is caused by infectious proteins. Hunters who are field dressing animals should not touch the brain or spinal fluids until the carcass has been declared disease free.

Cryptosporidiosis: A disease caused by a single-cell parasite found in the stool of wild animals that are infected. It causes serious flu-like symptoms. Human infection comes through contact with infected animal stool. Infected humans can transmit the disease in the same manner by coming in contact with the fecal matter of infected people.

Decay: As applied to the meat preservation process, decay is evident when the meat product is decomposing, or rotting away.

Degrees Fahrenheit: A temperature scale based on the work of German scientist Daniel G. Fahrenheit who lived from 1686 to 1726. On this temperature scale, water freezes at 32 degrees, and boils at 212 degrees.

Deer parapoxvirus: Affected animals have scabby and crusty lesions on their face, neck, and antlers. Hunters are infected when they nick their hands with knives during field dressing. Infected hunters will develop lesions on their hands.

Dry curing: A form of preserving meat that relies on naturally occurring microbiological processes that are initiated when the surface of meat is rubbed with a salt-based curing compound.

Dry cure box: A container large enough to pack a salt cure around meat products.

Drying: This is the process of removing moisture from meat by exposing the product to dry air or heat in a controlled environment.

E. coli: A bacteria that inhabits the intestinal tract of animals and humans. Meat is infected when it comes in contact with intestinal organs during slaughter. The disease causes serious illness with symptoms including bloody diarrhea. It is important to prevent cross contamination to other foods during cooking procedures.

Enzymes: The catalysts in the biological process that are used in the transformation of molecules.

Erythorbate: A derivative of erythorbic acid used commonly by commercial meat processors to maintain the red or pink color in meat.

Fahrenheit: A system of measuring temperature named after its inventor who was a German physicist.

Fat oxidation: When meat fats come in contact with oxygen, the color of the meat product will change to an undesirable color. This is a part of the spoilage process that will lead to the meat product having a rancid smell.

Fast freezing: The process of bringing food down to extremely cold temperatures as soon as possible to preserve freshness and enhance flavor.

Field dressing: The art of properly cleaning game harvested in the wild. This involves removing the internal organs, cleaning out the cavity, and possibly quartering the carcass for transportation in the case of a large animal like an elk.

Fryer: A chicken slaughtered at nine to 12 weeks weighing 3 or 4 pounds.

Formula-fed veal: This type of veal comes from calves that are slaughtered when they are 18 to 20 weeks old. The meat is ivory or creamy pink in color with a firm and fine appearance.

Free-raised veal: This type of veal comes from calves that are slaughtered when they are 24 weeks old. The calves are raised on their mother's milk and pasture grasses without the introduction of growth hormones or antibiotics. The meat is rich pink in color with a lower fat content than other types of veal.

Giardiasis: A disease caused by a microscopic parasite found in stools of domestic and wild animals. Symptoms of infection in humans appear one to two weeks after infection, and may last for two to six weeks.

Serious flu-like symptoms including stomach cramps and decreased appetite.

Giblets: The internal organs of poultry that are considered edible, such as the heart, liver, and gizzard.

Hot pack: This terminology describes the process of putting hot meat into canning jars just before they are placed in a pressure canner.

Ice tongs: Used to lift ice in and out of the icehouse or in the home delivery of ice blocks. Homeowners use smaller versions around the kitchen.

Knackwurst: A small sausage with German roots that may contain veal or pork.

Listeria monocytogenes: Discovered in 1981, it is spread when people fail to wash their hands after handling poultry. It can be controlled by proper refrigeration of poultry, and by frequent washing of hands when handling uncooked poultry.

Lyme disease: Spread by bites from deer ticks. The first indication of infection is a rash that looks like a bull's-eye at the point of the bite.

Nitrite or nitrate: These agents help the meat retain a red or pink color. It inhibits the growth of clostridium botulinum, which is a deadly microorganism.

Magnesium oxide: Used as an anti-caking element in dairy products and canned vegetables, and can be used as a medicinal laxative.

Maltodextrin: An easily digestible sugar starch used as a food additive to enhance the food. This agent has a taste much like sugar, and it is used as a thickening agent in sauces.

Meat preservation: This is the process of using salt and chemicals or heat to inhibit the growth of bacteria and pathogens in meat.

Meat thermometer: An instrument with a probe that allows you to measure the internal temperature of foods being cooked to ensure that food is heated to sufficient temperatures to kill disease-causing organisms.

Monosodium glutamate: Usually known as MSG; used to enhance the flavor of processed meats.

Mostaccioli noodles: Pasta tubes with ridges all the way around. The ends are cut at an angle.

Mutton: The meat from a sheep.

Non-formula-fed veal: This type of veal comes from calves that are slaughtered when they are 22 to 26 weeks old. This product is sold as "calf meat" in retail outlets. These calves are fed grain and hay in addition to milk. The meat is a darker red in color with some marbling and fat.

Pathogens: Organisms that are the cause of disease in humans.

Pemmican: A mixture of meat protein and fruit or berries used by early American Indians, which contains many essential nutrients.

Petcock: A valve on the lid of a pressure canner for controlling pressure in the canner.

Plague: Disease spread by fleas that come from rodents and other animals infected with the plague. Pneumonic plague is a serious illness that can be life threatening.

Prosciutto: A salt-cured ham that is usually sliced very thin when served.

Q fever: A bacteria found in sheep and goats. Birds and ticks also carry this disease. Humans can contract this disease by drinking unpasteurized dairy products.

Rancid: A smell of something that is rotting, such as meat fat.

Raw pack: This terminology describes the process of putting raw meat into canning jars just before they are placed in a pressure canner.

Refrigeration: The use of mechanical systems and chemical such as Freon to reduce the temperature of food sufficiently to inhibit the growth of dangerous bacteria.

Rocky Mountain spotted fever: Transmitted to people through tick bites. Flu-like symptoms appear in three to 14 days after infection, and may last for two to three weeks.

Rose veal: This type of veal comes from calves that are slaughtered when they are 35 weeks old and is available in the United Kingdom. The meat is pink in color.

Salmonellosis: Humans are infected by eating foods that are infected with the bacteria. Serious flu-like symptoms appear in eight to 72 hours after infection, and may last for four to seven days. People should avoid foods that have not been refrigerated properly.

Salt beef: Beef that has been cured using either a brine solution or dry packing process to preserve the meat. Salt beef usually does not remain in usable condition as long as salt pork.

Salt horse: Salt pork or salt beef that came to be known as salt horse because of the way it came packed for use on sailing ships.

Salt pork: Pork that has been cured using either a brine solution or dry packing process to preserve the meat.

Sanitize: To use heat or chemical action to sterilize a table or cooking utensil. Sterilization removes all hazardous pathogens.

Sausage casings: Tubes made from proteins that hold sausage in a shape that is acceptable to the retail market.

Shallots: From a plant that is related to the lily, and closely related to the onion. They have a milder flavor than garlic.

Showering: Finished summer sausages are placed in a cooler of cold water to release the heat and prevent shrinkage.

Smoking meat: The process of adding flavor to meat by exposing the product to wood smoke in an enclosed area at a controlled temperature. Smoking aids in the preservation process.

Sodium nitrate: This is a salt compound normally called saltpeter.

Sodium erythorbate: A sodium salt of erythorbic acid. It reduces nitric oxide in meat, which brings about a faster cure and helps meat to retain a pink color. It is produced from sugars derived from sugar beets, cane sugar, and corn. If consumed in excessive amounts, it is believed to be a carcinogen.

Sopressata: This is Italian dry-cured salami.

Sorbitol: A sugar-alcohol based sweetener used in various food products.

Staphylococcus: A microorganism found in foods improperly refrigerated, such as chicken salad. It can be carried on human hands, in nasal passages, or in human throats.

Sugar curing: During the curing process, sweeteners such as sugar or honey are added to the curing solution to add additional flavoring to the meat. There are specific temperature requirements to make this process successful.

Toxoplasmosis: Caused by a single-cell parasite. Humans are infected by eating raw or undercooked venison, lamb, or pork. Only eating food that has been properly cooked is the best defense against this disease.

Veal: Meat from calves butchered at a young age.

West Nile virus: This virus starts in wild bird populations and then is transmitted to humans by tick bites. Sudden bird die-offs in a certain area is a clue that the virus is present. People working and recreating in the outdoors should protect themselves from tick bites.

USDA Recipes for Canning Poultry, Red Meats, and Seafood

Chicken or Rabbit

Procedure: Choose freshly killed and dressed, healthy animals. Large chickens are more flavorful than fryers. Dressed chicken should be chilled for six to 12 hours before canning. Dressed rabbits should be soaked for one hour in water containing 1 tablespoon of salt per quart, and then rinsed. Remove excess fat. Cut the chicken or rabbit into suitable sizes for canning. Can with or without bones.

Hot pack — Boil, steam, or bake meat until about two-thirds done. Add 1 teaspoon salt per quart to the jar, if desired. Fill hot jars with pieces and hot broth, leaving 1 ¼-inch headspace. Remove air bubbles and adjust headspace if needed.

Raw pack — Add 1 teaspoon salt per quart, if desired. Fill hot jars loosely with raw meat pieces, leaving 1 ¼-inch headspace. Do not add liquid.

Wipe rims of jars with a dampened clean paper towel. Adjust lids and process.

Recommended process time for chicken or rabbit in a dial-gauge pressure canner			Canner pressure (PSI) at altitudes of			
Style of Pack	Jar Size	Process Time	0 to 2,001	2,001 to 4,000 ft	4,001 to 6,000 ft	6,001 to 8,000 ft
Without Bones: Hot and Raw	Pints	75 min	11 lb	12 lb	13 lb	14 lb
	Quarts	90 min	11 lb	12 lb	13 lb	14 lb
With Bones: Hot and Raw	Pints	65 min	11 lb	12 lb	13 lb	14 lb
	Quarts	75 min	11 lb	12 lb	13 lb	14 lb

Recommended process time for Chicken or Rabbit in a weighted-gauge pressure canner			Canner Pressure (PSI) at Altitudes of	
Style of Pack	Jar Size	Process Time	0 to 1,000 ft	Above 1,000 ft
Without Bones: Hot and Raw	Pints	75 min	10 lb	15 lb
	Quarts	90 min	10 lb	15 lb
With Bones: Hot and Raw	Pints	65 min	10 lb	15 lb
	Quarts	75 min	10 lb	15 lb

Ground or Chopped Meat

Bear, beef, lamb, pork, sausage, veal, venison

Procedure: Choose fresh, chilled meat. With venison, add one part high-quality pork fat to three or four parts venison before grinding. Use freshly made sausage, seasoned with salt and cayenne pepper (sage may cause a bitter off-flavor). Shape chopped meat into patties or balls or cut cased sausage into 3- to 4-inch links. Cook until lightly browned. Ground meat may be sautéed without shaping. Remove excess fat. Fill hot jars with pieces. Add boiling meat broth, tomato juice, or water, leaving 1-inch headspace. Remove air bubbles and adjust headspace if needed. Add 1 teaspoon of salt per quart to the jars, if desired. Wipe rims of jars with a dampened clean paper towel. Adjust lids and process.

Recommended process time for Ground or Chopped Meat in a dial-gauge pressure canner			Canner Pressure (PSI) at Altitudes of			
Style of Pack	Jar Size	Process Time	0 to 2,001	2,001 to 4,000 ft	4,001 to 6,000 ft	6,001 to 8,000 ft
Hot	Pints	75 min	11 lb	12 lb	13 lb	14 lb
	Quarts	90 min	11 lb	12 lb	13 lb	14 lb
Recommended process time for Ground or Chopped Meat in a weighted-gauge pressure canner			Canner Pressure (PSI) at Altitudes of			
Style of Pack	Jar Size	Process Time	0 to 1,000 ft		Above 1,000 ft	
Hot	Pints	75 min	10 lb		15 lb	
	Quarts	90 min	10 lb		15 lb	

Strips, Cubes, or Chunks of Meat

Bear, beef, lamb, pork, veal, venison

Procedure: Choose quality chilled meat. Remove excess fat. Soak strong-flavored wild meats for one hour in brine water containing 1 tablespoon of salt per quart. Rinse. Remove large bones.

Hot pack — Precook meat until rare by roasting, stewing, or browning in a small amount of fat. Add 1 teaspoon of salt per quart to the jar, if desired. Fill hot jars with pieces and add boiling broth, meat drippings, water, or tomato juice (especially with wild game), leaving 1-inch headspace. Remove air bubbles and adjust headspace if needed.

Raw pack — Add 1 teaspoon of salt per quart to the jar, if desired. Fill hot jars with raw meat pieces, leaving 1-inch headspace. Do not add liquid.

Wipe rims of jars with a dampened clean paper towel. Adjust lids and process.

Recommended process time for Strips, Cubes, or Chunks of Meat in a dial-gauge pressure canner			Canner Pressure (PSI) at Altitudes of			
Style of Pack	Jar Size	Process Time	0 to 2,001	2,001 to 4,000 ft	4,001 to 6,000 ft	6,001 to 8,000 ft
Hot and Raw	Pints	75 min	11 lb	12 lb	13 lb	14 lb
	Quarts	90 min	11 lb	12 lb	13 lb	14 lb
Recommended process time for Strips, Cubes, or Chunks of Meat in a weighted-gauge pressure canner			Canner Pressure (PSI) at Altitudes of			
Style of Pack	Jar Size	Process Time	0 to 1,000 ft		Above 1,000 ft	
Hot and Raw	Pints	75 min	10 lb		15 lb	
	Quarts	90 min	10 lb		15 lb	

Meat Stock (Broth)

Beef: Saw or crack fresh trimmed beef bones to enhance extraction of flavor. Rinse bones and place in a large stockpot or kettle, cover bones with water, add pot cover, and simmer three to four hours. Remove bones, cool broth, and pick off meat. Skim off fat, add meat trimmings removed from bones to broth, and reheat to boiling. Fill hot jars, leaving 1-inch headspace. Wipe rims of jars with a dampened clean paper towel. Adjust lids and process.

Chicken or turkey: Place large carcass bones (with most of meat removed) in a large stockpot, add enough water to cover bones, cover pot, and simmer 30 to 45 minutes or until remaining attached meat can be easily stripped from bones. Remove bones and pieces, cool broth, strip meat, discard excess fat, and return meat trimmings to broth. Reheat to boiling and fill jars, leaving 1-inch headspace. Wipe rims of jars with a dampened clean paper towel. Adjust lids and process.

Recommended process time for Meat Stock in a dial-gauge pressure canner			Canner Pressure (PSI) at Altitudes of			
Style of Pack	Jar Size	Process Time	0 to 2,001	2,001 to 4,000 ft	4,001 to 6,000 ft	6,001 to 8,000 ft
Hot	Pints	20 min	11 lb	12 lb	13 lb	14 lb
	Quarts	25 min	11 lb	12 lb	13 lb	14 lb
Recommended process time for Meat Stock in a weighted-gauge pressure canner			Canner Pressure (PSI) at Altitudes of			
Style of Pack	Jar Size	Process Time	0 to 1,000 ft		Above 1,000 ft	
Hot	Pints	20 min	10 lb		15 lb	
	Quarts	25 min	10 lb		15 lb	

Clams

Whole or minced

Procedure: Keep clams live on ice until ready to can. Scrub shells thoroughly and rinse, steam five minutes, and open. Remove clam meat. Collect and save clam juice. Wash clam meat in water containing 1 teaspoon of salt per quart. Rinse and cover clam meat with boiling water containing 2 tablespoons of lemon juice or ½ teaspoon of citric acid per gallon. Boil two minutes and drain. To make minced clams, grind clams with a meat grinder or food processor. Fill hot jars loosely with pieces and add hot clam juice and boiling water if needed, leaving 1-inch headspace. Remove air bubbles and adjust headspace if needed. Wipe rims of jars with a dampened clean paper towel. Adjust lids and process.

Recommended process time for Clams in a dial-gauge pressure canner			Canner Pressure (PSI) at Altitudes of			
Style of Pack	Jar Size	Process Time	0 to 2,001	2,001 to 4,000 ft	4,001 to 6,000 ft	6,001 to 8,000 ft
Hot	Half-pints	60 min	11 lb	12 lb	13 lb	14 lb
	Pints	70 min	11 lb	12 lb	13 lb	14 lb

Recommended process time for Clams in a weighted-gauge pressure canner			Canner Pressure (PSI) at Altitudes of	
Style of Pack	Jar Size	Process Time	0 to 1,000 ft	Above 1,000 ft
Hot	Half-pints	60 min	10 lb	15 lb
	Pints	70 min	10 lb	15 lb

King and Dungeness Crab Meat

It is recommended that blue crab meat be frozen instead of canned for best quality.

Crab meat canned according to the following procedure may have a distinctly acidic flavor and freezing is the preferred method of preservation at this time.

Procedure: Keep live crabs on ice until ready to can. Wash crabs thoroughly, using several changes of cold water. Simmer crabs 20 minutes in water containing cup of lemon juice and 2 tablespoons of salt (or up to 1 cup of salt, if desired) per gallon. Cool in cold water, drain, remove back shell, then remove meat from body and claws. Soak meat for two minutes in cold water containing 2 cups of lemon juice or 4 cups of white vinegar, and 2 tablespoons of salt (or up to 1 cup of salt, if desired) per gallon. Drain and squeeze crab meat to remove excess moisture. Fill hot half-pint jars with 6 ounces of crab meat and pint jars with 12 ounces, leaving 1-inch headspace. Add ½ teaspoon of citric acid or 2 tablespoons of lemon juice to each half-pint jar, or 1 teaspoon of citric acid or 4 tablespoons of lemon juice per pint jar. Cover with fresh boiling water, leaving 1-inch headspace. Remove air bubbles and adjust headspace if needed. Wipe rims of jars with a dampened clean paper towel. Adjust lids and process.

Recommended process time for King and Dungeness Crab Meat In a dial-gauge pressure canner			Canner Pressure (PSI) at Altitudes of			
Style of Pack	Jar Size	Process Time	0 to 2,001	2,001 to 4,000 ft	4,001 to 6,000 ft	6,001 to 8,000 ft
See above	Half-pints	70 min	11 lb	12 lb	13 lb	14 lb
	Pints	80 min	11 lb	12 lb	13 lb	14 lb

Recommended process time for King and Dungeness Crab Meat in a weighted-gauge pressure canner			Canner Pressure (PSI) at Altitudes of	
Style of Pack	Jar Size	Process Time	0 to 1,000 ft	Above 1,000 ft
See above	Half-pints	70 min	10 lb	15 lb
	Pints	80 min	10 lb	15 lb

Fish in Pint Jars

Blue, mackerel, salmon, steelhead, trout, and other fatty fish except tuna

Caution: Bleed and eviscerate fish immediately after catching, never more than two hours after they are caught. Keep cleaned fish on ice until ready to can.

Note: Glass-like crystals of struvite, or magnesium ammonium phosphate, sometime form in canned salmon. There is no way for the home canner to prevent these crystals from forming, but they usually dissolve when heated and are safe to eat.

Procedure: If the fish is frozen, thaw it in the refrigerator before canning. Rinse the fish in cold water. You can add vinegar to the water (2 tablespoons per quart) to help remove slime. Remove head, tail, fins, and scales; it is not necessary to remove the skin. You can leave the bones in most fish because the bones become very soft and are a good source of calcium. For halibut, remove the head, tail, fins, skin, and the bones. Wash and remove all blood. Refrigerate all fish until you are ready to pack in jars.

Split fish lengthwise, if desired. Cut cleaned fish into 3 ½-inch lengths. If the skin has been left on the fish, pack the fish skin out for a nicer appearance, or skin in for easier jar cleaning. Fill hot pint jars, leaving 1-inch headspace. Add 1 teaspoon of salt per pint, if desired. Do not add liquids. Carefully clean the jar rims with a clean, damp paper towel; wipe with a dry paper towel to remove any fish oil. Adjust lids and process. Fish in half-pint or 12-ounce jars would be processed for the same amount of time as pint jars.

Recommended process time for Fish in Pint Jars in a dial-gauge pressure canner			Canner Pressure (PSI) at Altitudes of			
Style of Pack	Jar Size	Process Time	0 to 2,001	2,001 to 4,000 ft	4,001 to 6,000 ft	6,001 to 8,000 ft
See above	Pints	100 min	11 lb	12 lb	13 lb	14 lb
Recommended process time for Fish in Pint Jars in a weighted-gauge pressure canner			Canner Pressure (PSI) at Altitudes of			
Style of Pack	Jar Size	Process Time	0 to 1,000 ft		Above 1,000 ft	
See above	Pints	100 min	10 lb		15 lb	

Fish in Quart Jars

Blue, mackerel, salmon, steelhead, trout, and other fatty fish except tuna

Note: Glass-like crystals of struvite, or magnesium ammonium phosphate, sometime form in canned salmon. There is no way for the home canner to prevent these crystals from forming, but they usually dissolve when heated and are safe to eat.

Caution: Bleed and eviscerate fish immediately after catching, never more than two hours after they are caught. Keep cleaned fish on ice until ready to can.

Procedure: If the fish is frozen, thaw it in the refrigerator before canning. Rinse the fish in cold water. You can add vinegar to the water (2 tablespoons per quart) to help remove slime. Remove head, tail, fins, and scales; it is not necessary to remove the skin. You can leave the bones in most fish because the bones become very soft and are a good source of calcium. For halibut, remove the head, tail, fins, skin, and the bones. Wash and remove all blood. Refrigerate all fish until you are ready to pack in jars.

Cut the fish into jar-length fillets or chunks of any size. The one-quart straight-sided mason-type jar is recommended. If the skin has been left on the fish, pack the fish skin out for a nicer appearance, or skin in for easier jar cleaning. Pack solidly into hot quart jars, leaving 1-inch headspace. If desired, run a plastic knife around the inside of the jar to align the product; this allows firm packing of fish.

For most fish, no liquid, salt, or spices need to be added, although seasonings or salt may be added for flavor (1 to 2 teaspoons salt per quart, or amount desired).

For halibut, add up to 4 tablespoons of vegetable or olive oil per quart jar if you wish. The canned product will seem moister. However, the oil will increase the caloric value of the fish.

Carefully clean the jar rims with a clean, damp paper towel; wipe with a dry paper towel to remove any fish oil. Adjust lids and process.

Processing Change for Quart Jars: The directions for operating the pressure canner during processing of quart jars are different from those for processing pint jars, so please read the following carefully. It is critical to product safety that the processing directions are followed exactly. When you are ready to process your jars of fish, add 3 quarts of water to the pressure canner. Put the rack in the bottom of canner and place closed jars on the rack. Fasten the canner cover securely, but do not close the lid vent. Heat the canner on high for 20 minutes. If steam comes through the open vent in a steady stream at the end of 20 minutes, allow it to escape for an additional ten minutes. If steam does not come through the open vent in a steady stream at the end of 20 minutes, keep heating the canner until it does. Then allow the steam to escape for an additional ten minutes to vent the canner. This step removes air from inside the canner so the temperature is the same throughout the canner.

The total time it takes to heat and vent the canner should never be less than 30 minutes. The total time may be more than 30 minutes if you have tightly packed jars, cold fish, or larger sized canners. For safety's sake, you must have a complete, uninterrupted 160 minutes (2 hours and 40 minutes) at a minimum pressure required for your altitude. Write down the time at the beginning of the process and the time when the process will be finished.

Recommended process time for Fish in Quart Jars in a dial-gauge pressure canner			Canner Pressure (PSI) at Altitudes of			
Style of Pack	Jar Size	Process Time	0 to 2,001	2,001 to 4,000 ft	4,001 to 6,000 ft	6,001 to 8,000 ft
Raw	Quarts	160 min	11 lb	12 lb	13 lb	14 lb

Recommended process time for Fish in Quart Jars in a weighted-gauge pressure canner			Canner Pressure (PSI) at Altitudes of	
Style of Pack	Jar Size	Process Time	0 to 1,000 ft	Above 1,000 ft
Raw	Quarts	160 min	10 lb	15 lb

Oysters

Procedure: Keep live oysters on ice until ready to can. Wash shells. Heat five to seven minutes in preheated oven at 400° F. Cool briefly in ice water. Drain, open shell, and remove meat. Wash meat in water containing ½ cup salt per gallon. Drain. Add ½ teaspoon salt to each pint, if desired. Fill hot half-pint or pint jars with drained oysters and cover with fresh boiling water, leaving 1-inch headspace. Remove air bubbles and adjust headspace if needed. Wipe rims of jars with a dampened clean paper towel. Adjust lids and process.

Recommended process time for Oysters in a dial-gauge pressure canner			Canner Pressure (PSI) at Altitudes of			
Style of Pack	Jar Size	Process Time	0 to 2,001	2,001 to 4,000 ft	4,001 to 6,000 ft	6,001 to 8,000 ft
See above	Half-pints or pints	75 min	11 lb	12 lb	13 lb	14 lb
Recommended process time for Oysters in a weighted-gauge pressure canner			Canner Pressure (PSI) at Altitudes of			
Style of Pack	Jar Size	Process Time	0 to 1,000 ft		Above 1,000 ft	
See above	Half-pints or pints	75 min	10 lb		15 lb	

Smoked Fish

Salmon, rockfish, and flatfish (sole, cod, flounder), and other fish

Caution: Safe processing times for other smoked seafoods have not been determined. Those products should be frozen. Smoking of fish should be done by tested methods. Lightly smoked fish is recommended for canning because the smoked flavor will become stronger and the flesh drier after processing. However, because it has not yet been cooked, do not taste lightly smoked fish before canning.

Follow these recommended canning instructions carefully. Use a 16 to 22 quart pressure canner for this procedure; do not use smaller pressure saucepans. Safe processing times have not been determined. Do not use jars larger than one pint. Half-pints could be safely processed for the same length of time as pints, but the quality of the product may be less acceptable.

Procedure: If smoked fish has been frozen, thaw in the refrigerator until no ice crystals remain before canning. If not done prior to smoking, cut fish into pieces that will fit vertically into pint canning jars, leaving 1-inch headspace. Pack smoked fish vertically into hot jars, leaving 1-inch headspace between the pieces and the top rim of the jar. The fish may be packed either loosely or tightly. Do not add liquid to the jars. Clean jar rims with a clean, damp paper towel. Adjust lids and process.

Processing Change for Smoked Fish: The directions for filling the pressure canner for processing smoked fish are different than those for other pressure canning, so please read the following carefully. It is critical to product safety that the processing directions are followed exactly. When you are ready to process your jars of smoked fish, measure 4 quarts (16 cups) of cool tap water and pour into the pressure canner. (**Note:** The water level probably will reach the screw bands of pint jars.) **Do not decrease the amount of water or heat the water before processing begins.** Place prepared, closed jars on the rack in the bottom of the canner, and proceed as with usual pressure canning instructions.

Recommended process time for Smoked Fish in a dial-gauge pressure canner			Canner Pressure (PSI) at Altitudes of			
Style of Pack	Jar Size	Process Time	0 to 2,001	2,001 to 4,000 ft	4,001 to 6,000 ft	6,001 to 8,000 ft
See above	Pints	110 min	11 lb	12 lb	13 lb	14 lb

Recommended process time for Smoked Fish in a weighted-gauge pressure canner			Canner Pressure (PSI) at Altitudes of	
Style of Pack	Jar Size	Process Time	0 to 1,000 ft	Above 1,000 ft
See above	Pints	110 min	10 lb	15 lb

Tuna

Tuna may be canned either precooked or raw. Precooking removes most of the strong-flavored oils. The strong flavor of dark tuna flesh affects the delicate flavor of white flesh. Many people prefer not to can dark flesh. It may be used as pet food.

Note: Glass-like crystals of struvite, or magnesium ammonium phosphate, sometime form in canned tuna. There is no way for the home canner to prevent these crystals from forming, but they usually dissolve when heated and are safe to eat.

Procedure: Keep tuna on ice until ready to can. Remove viscera and wash fish well in cold water. Allow blood to drain from stomach cavity. Place fish belly down on a rack or metal tray in the bottom of a large baking pan. Cut tuna in half crosswise, if necessary. Precook fish by baking at 250° F for two and one half to four hours (depending on size) or at 350° F for one hour. The fish may also be cooked in a steamer for two to four hours. If a thermometer is used, cook to a 165° to 175° F internal temperature. Refrigerate cooked fish overnight to firm the meat. Peel off the skin with a knife, removing blood vessels and any discolored flesh. Cut meat away from bones; cut out and discard all bones, fin bases, and dark flesh. Quarter. Cut quarters crosswise into lengths suitable for half-pint or pint jars. Fill into hot jars, pressing down gently to make a solid pack. Tuna may be packed in water or oil, whichever is preferred. Add water or oil to jars, leaving 1-inch headspace. Remove air bubbles and adjust headspace if needed. Add ½ teaspoon of salt per half-pint or 1 teaspoon of salt per pint, if desired. Carefully clean the jar rims with a clean, damp paper towel; wipe with a dry paper towel to remove any fish oil. Adjust lids and process.

Recommended process time for Tuna in a dial-gauge pressure canner			Canner Pressure (PSI) at Altitudes of			
Style of Pack	Jar Size	Process Time	0 to 2,001	2,001 to 4,000 ft	4,001 to 6,000 ft	6,001 to 8,000 ft
See above	Half-pints	100 min	11 lb	12 lb	13 lb	14 lb
Recommended process time for Tuna in a weighted-gauge pressure canner			Canner Pressure (PSI) at Altitudes of			
Style of Pack	Jar Size	Process Time	0 to 1,000 ft		Above 1,000 ft	
See above	Half-pints or pints	100 min	10 lb		15 lb	

Bibliography

Bison News. (2010, May 20). Retrieved May 20, 2010, from The National Bison Association: **www.bisoncentral.com/bison-news.php?s=&c=2 1&d=&e=&f=&g=&a=1434&w=2**

Blackburn, D. G. (2004). *Altitude Time and Pressure Adjustment Tables*. Retrieved May 13, 2010, from Canning USA.com: **http:// canningusa.com/IfICanYouCan/TechniqueAltitudeAdjustment. htm**

Bolton, B. (1996–2010). *How to Smoke Turkey-Smoked Turkey Tips*. Retrieved July 15, 2010, from What's Cooking America: **http:// whatscookingamerica.net/Poultry/smokingtips.htm**

Cargill Salt in San Francisco Bay. (2005). Retrieved June 16, 2010, from Cargill Salt: **www.cargill.com/cs/sf_bay/**

Changes in the Sheep Industry in the United States. (2008). Retrieved August 13, 2010, from The National Academies Report in Brief: **http://dels-old.nas.edu/dels/rpt_briefs/SheepFinal.pdf**

Christmas Treats. (n.d.). Retrieved July 8, 2010, from Gestgjafinn: **www. gestgjafinn.is/english/nr/356**

Disease Precautions for Hunters. (2010). Retrieved August 13, 2010, from The American Veterinary Association: **www.avma.org/public_ health/zoonotic_risks/hunters_precautions.asp**

Dunlay, W., & Kuhl, E. (1972). *Orleans Centennial.* Orleans, Nebraska: No longer in print or available.

Goats. (n.d.). Retrieved July 8, 2010, from Oklahoma State Univeristy Ag Facts: **http://oklahoma4h.okstate.edu/aitc/lessons/extras/facts/ goats.html**

Hunting and Fishing Licenses. (n.d.). Retrieved July 10, 2010, from Oklahoma Department of Wildlife Conservation: **www. wildlifedepartment.com/hflicens.htm**

Making a Dry-Curing Chamber. (2010). Retrieved May 15, 2010, from The Sausage Maker, Inc.: **www.sausagemaker.com/tutorials/ chamber/curing_chamber.html**

Marchello, M., & Garden-Robinson, J. (2004). *The Art and Practice of Sausage Making.* Retrieved July 10, 2010, from North Dakota State University Extension: www.ag.ndsu.edu/pubs/yf/foods/he176w.htm

Marianski, S., & Marianski, A. (2008). *The Art of Making Fermented Sausages.* Denver: Outskirts Press, Inc.

Marianski, S., Marianski, A., & Marianski, R. (2009). *Meat Smoking and Smokehouse Design.* Seminole Florida: Bookmagic, LLC.

McKinstry, G., Dawson, S., & Lorch, K. (n.d.). *Sausage Recipes.* Retrieved May 18, 2010, from Meet the 3 Men: **www.3men.com/sausage. htm#Summer Sausage**

Oster, E. W. (2010, July 12). Butchering Goats. (K. V. Oster, Interviewer)

Peterson, D. (1998). *Goat Milk: The Other White Milk*. Retrieved July 8, 2010, from Dairy Goat Journal: **www.dairygoatjournal.com/ issues/83/83-4/Daniel_Peterson.html**

Pyell, H. M. (2010, April 3). Member of Pioneer Family. (K. V. Oster, Interviewer)

Raabe, S. (2010, April 22). *Colorado: Bison Becoming the Other Red Meat*. Retrieved July 8, 2010, from Vail Daily: **www.vaildaily.com/ article/20100422/NEWS/100429838**

Ruhlman, M., & Polcyn, B. (2005). *Charcuterie*. New York: W.W. Norton & Company, Inc.

Sanitizing with Bleach. (n.d.). Retrieved April 1, 2010, from All QA Products: **www.allqa.com/ChlorineSanitizing.htm**

Sausage Stuffers. (2004–2010). Retrieved July 8, 2010, from The Sausage Maker, Inc: **www.sausagemaker.com/sausagestuffers.aspx**

Stanuszek, M. (n.d.). *Making a Dry-Curing Chamber*. Retrieved July 8, 2010, from The Sausage Maker, Inc: **www.sausagemaker.com/ tutorials/chamber/curing_chamber.html**

Tomaszewski, B. A. (2010, April 4). Owners of Tin Man Meats. (K. V. Oster, Interviewer)

Topics in Kansas History: Old West. (2010). Retrieved June 27, 2010, from Kansas State Historical Society: **www.kshs.org/research/topics/ oldwest/essay.htm**

Upland Game Birds. (2001–2010). Retrieved July 10, 2010, from Michigan Department of Natural Resources and Environment: **www.michigan. gov/dnr/0,1607,7-153-10363_10958---,00.html**

What is Chevon and Why Should I Eat It? (n.d.). Retrieved July 8, 2010, from International Kiko Goat Association, Inc.: **www.theikga.org/chevon.html**

Wildlife Resources Division Georgia's Alligator Hunting Season. (2010). Retrieved July 10, 2010, from The Georgia Department of Natural Resources: **www.georgiawildlife.com/node/610**

Wright, M. (2009). *Meat Curing at Home — The Setup.* Retrieved April 5, 2010, from Wrightfood: Recipes & Culinary Adventures From a Brit in Seattle: **http://mattikaarts.com/blog/charcuterie/meat-curing-at-home-the-setup/#comments**

Author Biography

Kenneth Oster is a 23-year veteran of the United States Air Force and is now serving as a substitute teacher. Kenneth has a bachelor's degree in educational studies from Western Governors University in Salt Lake City, Utah, and a doctorate in ministry from Great Plains Baptist Divinity School in Sioux Falls, South Dakota. Over the years, Kenneth and his wife, Joyce, have been involved in home canning and preserving a wide variety of fruits, vegetables, and meats for the enjoyment of their family. They have five children and 13 grandchildren.

Index

A

Alder, 31, 33

Alkaline phosphates, 29

Aluminum silicate, 257

Amino acid, 31

Ammonium carbonates, 31, 257

Antimicrobials, 31, 258

Apple, 31, 33, 160

B

Bacteriology, 24

Beef, 26-27, 29, 33, 48-49, 52, 55, 73, 92, 103-107, 109-110, 112-121, 123-124, 150-151, 155-156, 162, 169-170, 180, 191-193, 195, 197, 201, 203, 205, 216, 219-221, 248, 250, 251, 261, 267, 269-271

Botulism, 29, 56, 207-208

Brine, 28, 31, 34-35, 41, 228, 230-232, 240, 242-243, 69-70, 72, 75-76, 78-87, 94, 116, 138, 148,